EVANGELINEDROWNING

a dramatic work by
Kurt Gerard Heinlein

with music composed by
Katy Pfaffl

authorHOUSE®

AuthorHouse™
1663 Liberty Drive
Bloomington, IN 47403
www.authorhouse.com
Phone: 1-800-839-8640

No duplications or performances are permitted without contractual permission.

Published by AuthorHouse 4/5/2013

ISBN: 978-1-4817-2737-2 (sc)
ISBN: 978-1-4817-2736-5 (e)

Library of Congress Control Number: 2013904786

Cover photo by Elena Kalis

This book is printed on acid-free paper.

Because of the dynamic nature of the Internet, any web addresses or links contained in this book may have changed since publication and may no longer be valid. The views expressed in this work are solely those of the author and do not necessarily reflect the views of the publisher, and the publisher hereby disclaims any responsibility for them.

Project Development

Evangeline Drowning is the artistic culmination of extensive research and on-site interviews in Southeast Louisiana. Those interviewed include individuals from many walks of life, embodying variances in culture, age, political posturing, and socio-economic status. Intentional care was taken to interview people from multiple perspectives of the issues explored within the play. Some components of the text are derived from interview material and others are dramatically re-developed from factual accounts. Names have been changed to protect the identities of those interviewed. Development was funded by a Missouri State University Futures Grant titled *Vanishing Wetlands, Vanishing Cultures.* PI, Dr. Kurt Heinlein. Co-PI, Dr. Inno Onwueme.

Acknowledgements

Gratitude to Missouri State University, most notably The College of Arts & Letters, The Department of Theatre & Dance, and The Office of the Provost. Special thanks is also due to those who contributed unselfishly to the creation of this work: Carey Adams, Angela Anderson, Jared Arseman, Barataria Terrebonne Estuary Program, Ruth Barnes, The Bayou Playhouse, Michelle Benoit, Tab Benoit (Voice of the Wetlands), Mark Biggs, Randy Cheramie, The City of New Orleans Office of the Mayor, Dr. Craig Colten, Joel Cornwell, Mary Curole, Windell Curole, Brenda Dardar Robichaux, Alan Daugherty, Mark Davis, Department of Wildlife & Fisheries, Bernadette Dugas, Hannah Duncan, Dusenberry Family, Melissa Fagan, Elizabeth Mara Finder, Rev. Jerome Escasa, Jim Fields, Ariel Forste, Michael Frizzell, Rachel Gholson, Lorna Gianelloni, Jason Goff, David Guidry, Christopher Hallowell, Tessa Harbaugh, Courtney Heinlein, Leighton Heinlein, Sutton Heinlein, Dr. Patrick Hesp, Traci Hoover, Hotel St. Pierre, Dr. Oliver Houck, Becca Howes, Jonna Howes, Drew Irwin, Laura Jenkins, Kanome Jones, Adam Joyce, Karissa Kary, KMSU Radio, Marnie Liesel, C.C. Lockwood, Louisiana State University Department of Theatre, Maggie Marlin-Hess, Perry Martin, Dr. Belinda McCarthy, Sean McEwen, Bill McKibben, Dr. Doug Meffert, Hennesy Melancon, Cody Mobley, National Public Radio, Dr. Inno Onwueme, Original Cast and Production Team, Kristen Orr Henderson, Stacy Parker-Joyce, Glen Pitre, Kathy Randels, Renee Rhodes, Dr. Robin Roberts, Marsy Robinson, Capt. Ginger Rushing, Office of General Thomas Sands, Julie Schaper, Carly Schneider, Amanda Shaw, Mark Shexnayder, Cecilia Sirigos, Kristin Sosnowsky, South Lafourche High School, South Lafourche Middle School, Southern Repertory Theatre, Shelly Sparks, Kerry St. Pe, Vastine Stabler, Nick Stephens, Randy Stewart,

Dr. Jennifer Stoessner, Dr. Robert Thomas, Dr. Michael Tick, Mike Tidwell, Sam Valentine, Dr. Ivor Van Heerden, Andy Venneman, Dr. Les Wade, Sarah Wiggin, Andy Willadson, Dr. Bob Willenbrink, and Wendy Wilson Billiot. Many of those interviewed in the development of the play have chosen to remain anonymous. Heartfelt thanks for opening your doors and your lives, and for entrusting me with your story.

Author's Introduction

2008. I was finalizing my dissertation for a doctorate in theatre from Louisiana State University. Titled *Green Theatre*, my goal for the dissertation was to contribute to the small foundation of research that legitimizes the arts as a measurable form for implementing social change, notably social betterment that is specific to environmental issues. I made two definitive early discoveries in my doctoral research. First, that treating socio-environmental issues on stage in a manner that engages audiences is no easy task. Second, that there was (and still is) an extremely small body of plays successfully dramatizing socio-environmental issues. The dramatic works out there were limited mostly to children's plays, one person performance pieces, and street theatre. While all three are important performance formats, this pointed to the fact that there was virtually no canon of commercially viable plays that explored socio-environmental issues-nothing for an ensemble cast that could be produced for audiences in colleges, high schools, and professional theatres around the nation. "This is a tremendous problem," I thought. Theatre is the "immediate art," it is the "reactionary art," it is the art, which I was arguing in my dissertation, that has the power to engage the imagination, reach inside of our identity constructs, and re-orient the way we perceive the world. Yet, there was essentially no body of green plays that were available to be produced? I reflected upon an interview that environmental theatre pioneer Theresa May had conducted with Zelda Fichandler. During the interview, Fichandler (Artistic Director of Arena Stage) stated, "I would love to do green plays, but where are they?"

It was a vital question, and a decade later, there was still no answer. Fichandler, of course, had to consider a host of questions in choosing individual works for the Arena Stage season. Would the work be commercially viable? Would audiences enjoy it? How would it compliment the season? Can it be cast? How much would it cost to produce? Would it have a life beyond Arena Stage? After all, as impassioned as Fichandler may have been about environmental betterment, she had a theatre to run, a board to please, audiences to entertain, and a budget to keep in the black. My own experiences inform me that social drama is anything but the "go to" genre for drawing audiences into a theatrical season.

Thus, a seed was planted for this journey toward the development of *Evangeline Drowning*. I was arriving at the fact that if I were to put my art where my mouth is, I had try to develop a new, commercially viable play that addressed green issues. My dissertation *Green Theatre* was published as a book shortly thereafter, furthering the need to "put up or shut up." I had to at least try my damndest. Write a play. Begob. A *green* play that held potential for production by colleges, professional theatres, and high schools. A play that audiences could enjoy. A play that would embrace audiences, not alienate them, and allow them to consider the environmental issues within. A tall task? Without question, even for the experienced playwright, which I definitively was not. I was an actor, a theatre movement and stunt guy, who just hacked out a doctoral dissertation and was lucky enough that someone wanted to print it as a book. I had never even considered writing a play.

I revisited an online article written by Bill McKibben titled, *Imagine That, What the Warming World Needs Now is Art Sweet Art*. McKibben's article notes some of the challenges in addressing environmental issues in artistic form. Importantly, it also serves as an impassioned plea for artists to embrace the issues at hand. It begins:

> "Shall I compare thee to climate change? Here's the paradox: if the scientists are right, we're living through the biggest thing that's happened since human civilization emerged. One species, ours, has by itself in the course of a couple of generations managed to powerfully raise the

temperature of an entire planet, to knock its most basic systems out of kilter. But oddly, though we know about it, we don't *know* about it. It hasn't registered in our gut; it isn't part of our culture. Where are the books? The poems? The plays?"

The article served as a timely re-affirmation of my own argument in *Green Theatre*, supporting the notion that the arts can positively impact societal change. It also reminded me that I *had* to try to write this play. But how? About what? How could a novice playwright possibly take this on? How could I dramatically treat the scope of green issues in a manner that kept the story focused, interesting, and emotionally relatable? Having lived in Louisiana for half a decade, I had a sense the Gulf region could be a starting point, but all I really knew was that I damned well wanted some kind of answer for Fichandler's inquiry. As I reflected upon the task ahead, I revisited a 2006 interview I had conducted with McKibben during my doctoral research. One of his responses jumped out:

> Heinlein: In your article *Imagine That*, you mention "unsettling the audience" as well as the notion of "hope." How do you feel artists and theatre practitioners can manage to treat the issue of climate change without alienating audiences?
>
> McKibben: I don't know. That's why I'm not a theatre artist. But I'd start with Katrina somehow.

There it was again. Some water for the seed. South Louisiana. A region which long before Hurricane Katrina (and unbeknownst to many) had become a portal for examining the relationship between our environmental behaviors and their impact upon society. It was (and still is) a hotbed for viewing the complicated intermingling of politics, industry, ecology, and our social systems. I was keenly aware of the multitude of excellent literary and artistic works that were being developed about post-Katrina New Orleans, and had no interest in duplicating those in dramatic form. Ironically, what I *wasn't* seeing in the new works, or in the news or political dialogues, was a conversation about the elephant in the room. The elephant was green, and it was sitting amidst the political, industrial, and socio-environmental behaviors that heightened the damage and loss of life during Katrina. *Why was nobody talking about it?* Why was nobody discussing the practices that led to wetlands loss and the consequent increase in surge and hurricane damage upon South Louisiana? Why was no one talking about the wetland areas south of New Orleans where cultures and lives were being devastated by preventable land loss? There was certainly lots of post-Katrina banter and finger pointing about levees and urban reconstruction costs, but it seemed that all but an enlightened few knew of or focused upon the socio-ecological issues that underscored and expounded Katrina's devastation.

I soon found myself working with Dr. Inno Onwueme, an agronomist and Associate Dean within the College of Natural and Applied Sciences at Missouri State University. As a duo, we were an unlikely coupling- an agronomist and an actor. Add a priest or rabbi to our mix and it would have made the beginning of a great joke. Together, however, we earned a notable Futures Grant from Missouri State in order to investigate and address these very wetland issues. Titled *Vanishing Wetlands, Vanishing Cultures*, the aim of the three-year grant project was tri-fold: 1. Research the issues of wetlands loss in South Louisiana and the consequent disintegration of historic cultures. 2. Conduct a wide host of interviews with individuals in the region. 3. Construct a new theatre work that treated the topic, with an original production to be held at Missouri State University. Thrilled at this nod of financial and moral support from MSU for our initiative, I quickly found myself thinking, "How on earth am I now going to write a play about these issues that someone wants to watch?"

Extensive time was spent interviewing a broad spectrum of individuals in South Louisiana. We interviewed fishermen, shrimpers, clergy, aid workers, politicians, authors, environmentalists, oil workers, homemakers, scientists, educators, artists, community activists, military personnel, musicians, and numerous others. We interviewed individuals from an array of ages, races, and socio-economic backgrounds. We interviewed individuals with a multitude of political perspectives and outlooks regarding the causes of, and solutions for, wetlands loss and cultural disintegration. However, after a full year into the interviews I still found myself searching for a focused play topic. Ironically, I actually felt further from identifying a central theme than ever. I knew I needed a story, a very *human* story to focus on within the depth of these very complicated issues. But, there were *so many* stories, so many varying perspectives, and so many ideas for solutions, that ultimately, it seemed logistically impossible to find a means to uniformly address them in dramatic form. After all, the issues at hand spanned politics, economics, socio-environmental practices, cultural disintegration, and the profound losses experienced by many residents of South Louisiana. In short, I was discovering first-hand the inherent difficulties in dramatizing socio-environmental issues.

I took this impasse as an opportunity to step back and consider the breadth of our interviews. In doing so, I noted two unifying elements that seemed to emerge in all of the dialogues. First, most parties seemed to agree about the *causes* of wetlands loss in South Louisiana and the notion that they needed to be addressed. Few, however, appeared to agree about the potential solutions. In relation, every positive idea for a solution seemed to hold a potentially negative impact for a second or third social party. Second, there was clearly little effective wide-scale (state or national) communication on the issues. The issues, feelings, and experiences ran so very deep that there appeared to be very little constructive cross-perspective dialogue that would result in betterment. I remember thinking frequently during the interviews, "If I could only get all these good people in one room." If only…

Shortly after, Dr. Onwueme accepted a Provost position at a university in Pennsylvania. Flying solo, I visited several schools in

Lafourche Parish and (with much gratitude toward administrators and open-minded parents) was allowed to interview several groups of teenage students. I still had no primary focus for the play. Unbeknownst to me, I would be forever changed by what I was to uncover in the dialogues. The first thing that stuck me during the interviews was that the students seemed to have a rare and unique clarity on the complex matters at hand. That clarity included the possession of an uncannily mature knowledge of the issues. Simultaneously, the students seemed to hold few personal motives or political objectives to color their responses. In contrast, they provided a well of profound relevant experiences and a great willingness to share their formidable stories. I often found myself caught off guard by the advanced vocabulary and life wisdom contained in their discussions, which seemed an odd counterbalance to the more predictable displays of teen angst and school social drama. The more I conversed with the students, the more it became clear that they talked very little about experiences germane to these issues in the course of their daily lives. Ironically, in response to my questions posed as an "outsider" (a student's words, not mine) they were open, available, candid, and forthright. As cliché as it sounds, we shared many laughs and even a few tears. It became overwhelmingly clear to me that these young people had experienced financial hardship, profound social difficulties, and were witnessing the imminent decay of family and vital cultural heritage. Many had been displaced, had their education trajectory sidetracked, and some played witness as friends and family lost lives in the wake of diminishing wetlands and corresponding hurricane activity. During our conversations, I often found myself in simultaneous awe and horror; in awe of their unprecedented honestly and unflinching resilience, and horrified that no one was telling their story.

2013. There is now a play, and yes, you will find if you choose to read onward that it was born inside a Lafourche Parish classroom. There have now been productions and readings and a tour. As the author, I really can't speak to its success or lack thereof regarding goals for commercial viability, building research foundations, and the lofty ideas this novice playwright had that helped plant a seed for creation. You may appreciate the play, or it may drive you to drink. I only hope, that it provides some small window of opportunity for you to pay witness to the young voices within, notably as our nation continues to search for ways to communicate about viable solutions.

Production History

Evangeline Drowning was first produced at Missouri State University. Following its inaugural run, the production toured to The Bayou Playhouse (Lockport, LA), Southern Repertory Theatre Crosstown Series (New Orleans, LA), and Swine Palace at Louisiana State University (Baton Rouge, LA). The cast and production design team were as follows:

Narrator .... *Adam Joyce*
Celia .... *Rachel Goodwin*
Tricia .... *Jessica Morgan*
Renee .... *Camille Claire Hendricks*
Jackie .... *Drew Maestas*
Thomas .... *Brandt Shields*
Dru .... *Margaret Howard*
JD ....*Rolando Rodriguez*
Ronnie .... *Rachel Flanigan*
Chad .... *Taylor Paul*
Sonya .... *Samantha Long*
Roxannne .... *Marnie Liesel*
LeDeux .... *Josh Watford*
Thoreau .... *Matt Tassell*
Michelle ....*Rebecca Yi*
Saranda .... *Laura Jenkins*
Tice .... *Joel Cornwell*
Girl ....*Veronica Schlette*

Producers .... *Mark Biggs, Robert Willenbrink*
Scenic Design .... *Robert Little*
Costume Design .... *Louise M. Herman*
Lighting Design .... *Ethan Steimel*
Marketing Director .... *Mark Templeton*

Sound Design.. *Mark Putman*
Stage Manager .... *Katie Rogers*
Assistant Director .... *Nathan McVay*
Assistant Stage Manager......................... *Kacey Monke*
Technical Director .... *Christopher DePriest*
Videography/Film Editing......................... *Adam Joyce*
Music Director .... *Jessica Morgan*
Voice-Overs... *Randy Stewart*
Documentarian .... *Taylor Horst*

Casting and Dialect

The ensemble of actors should be representative of the diversity of cultures contained within South Louisiana. However, to provide flexibility in casting, the heritage of most characters is not provided. For many of the characters, ethnicity is flexible and should be attended to in the casting process with the key notion that some cultural diversity is essential to the intent of the work. In relation, many South Louisiana dialects are extremely difficult to perform, born out of the cultural-linguistic gumbo that makes up the region. Dialects may be utilized in production, but please not at the expense of honest and relatable characters. The play, without exception, should be centered on the experiences of the characters as relatable to American culture at large, achievable through honest and relatable portrayals. At no time should the performance of the actor(s) in their attempt at dialect or feigned cultural authenticity take focus from the main tenant of the work, notably the experience of shared human emotions as inspired by moment-to-moment discovery of character journey.

Youth and Educational Productions

The author grants permission for authorized productions at high schools and theatrical venues utilizing youth actors to make necessary changes to the "adult language" contained within. If changes are made, full effort should be given to preserving the dynamic of the dialogue and the author's intent. Other than the removal or change of "adult language," permission is not granted to make other changes to the text or music.

Green Initiative
In line with the original production and the author's intent, it is recommended that efforts be made by producing companies toward a green production initiative, including the utilization of recycled scenic and costume elements.

Time and Place
Aside from the concrete determinations of pre and post-hurricane, notions of time and place are contemporary but variable. The dialogue moves from moment to moment and place to place as dictated by emotional journey, not sequential or linear logic. The absence of specific determinations of places and socio-environmental phenomena (names of hurricanes, etc.) is intentional, aimed at allowing the text to provide more direct and personal relevance to readers and audience members outside the Gulf region and to avoid polarizing limitations as a singular "event" play.

Characters

(With the exception of the Narrator and Child, all characters are high school students.)

Narrator	Thirties. Female or male. A dramatist and research project coordinator.
Celia	Extremely reserved. A budding writer. Working on a contemporary children's adaptation of Longfellow's *Evangeline*.
Tricia	A vibrant vocalist/guitarist. An activist via her music, which also serves as her tool for self-reflection.
Renee	Popular. Daughter of a wealthy family and conservative state politician.
Jackie	The son and grandson of Zydeco musicians. Energetic. Funny. The self-labeled future CEO of Sony Entertainment.
Thomas	Future Catholic Priest. Son of a fifth generation Catholic-Cajun family.
Dru	Self-described anarchist. Daughter of an oil executive, yet loathes all things corporate. Finds comfort in the piano.
JD	Houma Indian. Son of a shrimping family turned oil employees.
Ronnie	Granddaughter of a noted community activist. She is also a budding activist.
Chad	Fourth generation military family. Enlisted. Will be deployed following high school graduation.

Sonya	Friendly. Popular. A volunteer at a hospital in town. Referred to as "Mother Teresa" by her friends.
Roxanne	Rescuer of all things four-legged. Head of the drama club. Quirky. Energetic.
LeDeux	Sixth generation crabber. His family dabbles in construction and gator tours. Competitive baseball player.
Thoreau	Moved from Michigan at age seven. Son of a hurricane researcher. Intelligent. A self-described "sensible-environmentalist." Could be cast as female.
Michelle	From a sixth generation Asian merchant family. Educational goals beyond high school at conflict with her concern for local family.
Saranda	A dedicated young mother. Her fiancé is currently on an oil vessel.
Tice	Hip. Offbeat. A budding young photographer.
Child	A girl. Approximately eight to ten years of age.

Place: Gulf Coast, LA. Lafourche Parish.
Act I: Pre-Hurricane.
Act II: Post Hurricane.

EVANGELINE DROWNING
Act I

(Lights up. Narrator enters, speaks to audience.)

Narrator   Six months after a final interview visit to Lafourche and Terrebonne parishes, I found myself sitting in a coffee house perusing notes for the construction of this play. If anything was learned during my year of interviews there, it was that the issues of wetlands loss in the region are unbelievably complicated, made more profound by the deep emotional and cultural connection between the people and their region. The *key facts* are simple. The South Louisiana wetlands are disappearing at a profound rate. Every hour a football field size of land is lost forever to the Gulf of Mexico, a process unarguably connected to man-made activity and industry. As a result, many people of South Louisiana are losing their land, their homes, their communities, their economy, their cultures, and in some cases, their lives. As concrete as these facts are, both the causes and potential solutions are extraordinarily complicated, clouded amidst variations in environmental outlook and a whirlwind of finger-pointing, corporate agendas, economic allegiances, and political mudslinging. During my visits, without fail I witnessed both the profound loss and unbreakable pride of the people in the region. That loss and pride have grown inseparable, creating the essence of a people with an impenetrable historical bond, but an uncertain future. I often found myself asking, "How can this be happening? How the *hell* can this be happening?! How the hell can this be happening *here*? How... in the U.S? Where is the damned help?"

Or...in contrast, I often found myself trying to shut out the less politically correct thoughts... "Should there even be help? Is it too late? Should the people in this region just leave while they can...if they can? In light of the horrific human errors that created this mess, do we chalk it up to learning experience and move onward? Why save this land? Why save these cultures?"

I felt completely incapable of translating these issues to the dramatic page. How can issues so complicated, so broad, and so emotionally explosive be contained within one play? Who is the antagonist? All of us? Everyone who uses oil and petroleum products? Everyone who eats Gulf seafood? Me? You? The government? Corporate America? How do I possibly write a play on socio-environmental issues that have causes and solutions that aren't even resolvable in *my own* mind?

I sat in that coffee shop surrounded by research documents and interview notes that detailed hundreds of stories of struggle and survival. I looked down and noted an unfamiliar piece of paper protruding from a folder. It was lined. The frays still attached from a spiral notebook. *(Pulls out paper kept folded inside a pocket notebook.)* In the top left corner, the words "Social Studies" had been scratched out. Below that, written in bubbly teenage print, was a letter. It read:

(Reading aloud.) "I'm sorry I didn't speak up when you talked to our class. Sometimes I think

if I open my mouth I'll cry or scream or both. So I just shut up. Thank you for asking us how we are doing. No one asks. We're not well. Things are bad. And please make people understand that we are not stupid. We're really nice people. I think people must not know what is happening to us or they would help. Right? *(Unseen, CC speaks the last lines of the letter with the Narrator.)* Please get people to help. Also, can I be in your play? 'Heart', CC."

I remembered her vividly from a visit to a high school in Lafourche Parish. Her teacher said she was working on a new children's adaptation of Longfellow's *Evangeline*. Only vaguely familiar with the story, I picked up a copy and discovered that *Evangeline* is an epic poem about two young Acadian lovers, torn apart by the unjust consequences of cultural and social politics. *(Recalling CC.)* CC. A shy junior sitting in a back corner of the room, a retroesque Care Bears rainbow t-shirt, and not one word said during my discussion with her class. Her letter, however, offered a timely reminder of the voices that are being lost in this socio-environmental crisis we've built for ourselves… those of our children, our youth. It is those voices who just may literally hold the future of the world in their hands. This play is their story. Not mine. Thank you, CC… and guess what? You are in the play. Act One.

(Blackout.)

(A soft special rises on a child. She is barely visible. She sings a gentle, broken, a capella version of "Through it All.")

Child   I hope to find you
               on a glowing summer day,

walking beside me
as the shadows fade away,
and as the days pass
and the summer turns to fall,
I hope to find you with me through it all.

*(Blackout on the child. She exits. Still in blackout, familiar
children's songs, nursery rhymes, and game lyrics begin.
They softly layer in, one by one. They start to build very
slowly. The verses repeat, each time gaining volume and
ferocity. As volume increases, the unseen voices begin
to move to the stage. As the voices travel, they begin to
interject various pleas and cries for help encountered
during the crisis moments of a hurricane. The audience is
surrounded by sounds of desperation and lost youth. The
actors can develop these phrases as they see fit according
to character. Each actor should only have a few phrases
that are repeated throughout until the final crescendo.)*

Ensemble   We're in here!
            Please God!
            Get inside!
            My God.
            It's a baby.
            I'm afraid.
            Get in the attic!
            Where's the dog!
            I'm not going without the fucking dog!
            I'm thirsty!
            You're hurting me.
            Get in the fucking car!
            No!
            Hurry up!
            We're out of gas!
            Leave it!
            God help us.
            Get in the car now!
            The phone is dead!

The road is blocked.
There's no gas.
Where's grandma?
Daddy!!
Help!
Etc, etc!

(Still in blackout, the cacophony reaches violent proportions as all voices arrive on stage. After a unified scream they stop abruptly. Silence. A special rises on Tricia, who is working on an acoustic version of "Saints.")

Tricia   We are trav'ling in the steps
of those who've gone before,
and we'll all be reunited,
on a new and sunlit shore.
Oh, when the saints go marching in.
Oh, when the saints go marching in.
Lord, how I want to be in that number,
when the saints go marching in...

(Lights rise gently and we discover the cast of characters in a DS line of tableaus, backs to the audience. As each is introduced, she/he turns to the audience and speaks. The dialogue is underscored by Tricia's song.)

Narrator   *(To audience.)* Pre- Hurricane.

Tricia   *(Sings.)* And when the sun, refuse to shine,
and when the moon turns red with blood.
Lord, how I want to be in that number,
when the moon turns red with blood.
Oh, when the people sound their call.
Oh, when the people sound their call.
Lord, how I want to be in that number,
when the people sound their call.
Some say this sinking land of trouble,
is the only one we need,
but I'm waiting for that morning,

when the new world is revealed.
Oh, when the new world is revealed.
Oh, when the new world is revealed.
Lord, how I want to be in that number,
when the new world is revealed.
Oh, when the saints go marching in.
Oh, when the saints go marching in.
Lord, how I want to be in that number,
when the saints go marching in.
And when the children sound their call.
And when the children sound their call.
Lord how I want to be in that number,
when the children sound their call.

Celia   *(Over Tricia's song.)* Once upon a time…

Narr   There was a young writer named Celia….

(Celia writes, re-interpreting Longfellow's opening verses of Evangeline. She will continue to write and read throughout the play, only sometimes interacting with others or engaging in ensemble activities. However, she has a strong connection with JD throughout.)

Celia   Once upon a time

Narr   There was a budding young singer named Tricia…

(Tricia continues to play.)

Celia   In a wetland primeval

Narr   And Renee. Cheerleader. Daughter of a state politician.

Renee   Straight A student…former. *(Her grades have dropped.)*

Celia   The murmuring oaks and naked cypress

Narr   Jackie. Son and grandson of noted Zydeco musicians.

Jackie	Future CEO of Sony Entertainment, bitches.
Celia	Once bearded with moss
Narr	Thomas. Future Priest.
Thomas	…and fifth generation Louisiana Cajun.
Celia	And in garments green
Narr	Dru. Daughter of an oil executive and self-described anarchist.
Dru	*(Dru joyfully gives the finger.)*
Celia	Now skeletal in the twilight
Narr	JD. Son of a Houma Nation leader. Friend to many.
JD	"The shadow which swims across the marsh and loses itself in the sunset." *(A joke acknowledging the misperceived mysticism of his Houma Indian heritage.)*
Celia	*(Smiles at JD. Speaks while looking at him.)* Stand proud and stubborn like dying cultures of old
Narr	Ronnie. Granddaughter of a noted community activist.
Ronnie	Hi.
Celia	With voices sad and prophetic
Narr	Chad. Son of an Army Captain. Fourth generation military.
Chad	Deploying for duty in June.
Celia	While the deep voiced creatures within
Narr	Sonya. Hospital volunteer. Called Mother Teresa by her friends.

Sonya	*(To Narrator.)* Oh Lord. Isn't she dead?
Celia	Sing a guttural funeral march
Narr	Roxanne. Head of the Drama Club. Savior of all things four-legged.
Roxanne	*(Joking.)* Canis-Humanicus-Dramaticus.
Celia	The encroaching Gulf also speaks
Narr	LeDeux. Sixth generation Louisiana Cajun.
LeDeux	…kick-ass second baseman and 'roid-free long-ball hitter. *(Flexes and laughs.)*
Celia	And in accents disconsolate answers their wails
Narr	Thoreau. Son of a scientist at the Hurricane Research Center.
Thoreau	Born in Michigan. Re-born in Da Bayou!
Celia	This is the wetlands primeval, proudly dying
Narr	Michelle. From a family of sixth generation merchants.
Michelle	*(Puts on her glasses.)* Hello.
Celia	And here are the hearts that within it live
Narr	Saranda. An impassioned young mother. Fiancé of a Gulf oil worker.
Saranda	*(Showing a picture.)* …and this is my little boy, Aiden Michael.
Celia	They now leap like the fawn when they hear the call of the Gulf
Narr	And Tice. A budding photojournalist.

(Tice takes a photo of self. Tricia stops playing.)

Tice   Ok guys, jump in.

*(The ensemble clumps together for a group picture.
General improvisation.)*

Tice   Say cheese.

All   Merde!

*(Tice takes the picture. On the flash, the group freezes in
tableau. After a beat, Celia breaks out of the tableau.)*

Celia   …and here are the hearts that lie within it

Narr   Once upon a time…

*(During Celia's following dialogue, the actors break
tableau one by one and methodically, slowly but with
emotional purpose, move to their places around the stage
for the top of the group dialogue that follows.)*

Celia   Once upon a time…
            This was the home of the Acadian Farmer
            The Indian Fisherman
            Of many cultures, proud and sufficient
            Of lives and love and bonds unbreakable
            Men and women whose lives glided on
            like the bayous that line the wetlands
            Now darkened by the shadows
            of a destructive new world
            But still reflecting an image of God's Heaven

            Drowning are those pleasant farms,
            and falling are the proud cypress
            The cultures within them forever departing
            Scattered like dust and leaves
            when the mighty blasts of August seize them
            And whirl them aloft
            and sprinkle them far over distant lands
            Tradition struggles to surface
            and breathes a willful breath

Yet he who believes in affection that hopes,
and endures, and is patient
She who believes in the strength
of human resilience and the beauty of
God given love
List to this mournful tradition still sung by…
(She thinks.)…sung by the children of this land
List to a tale of love in Acadie, home of the brave.

Narr   Once upon a time.

Ensemble Once upon a time.

    (Celia sits and continues to write.)

Narr   *(To ensemble.)* Can you give me a sense of what it's
like to grow up here?

Dru   You want the glossy color version or the fucked up
black and white?

Tice   Nothing's black and white. *(Takes a picture.)*

Dru   Nothing.

Narr   I want what you want me to know.

Dru   Don't be sure.

Chad   *(Joking.)* You really want this can of worms?

Narr   Yes.

Chad   Oh crap. Folgers coffee can about to open up.

Renee   You are such a dork.

Chad   No, I'm not, but Jo is. Do you know Jo? I hooked up
with her once. You know Jo…Jo Mama!

Narr   Can I use that?

Chad   Cool. Use it…like I used her mama! *(Laughs.)*

Renee	Oh my God. *(Turns to Narrator.)* Please help us.
Michelle	Please, this is serious.
JD	Be serious.
Renee	He's actually nice. He hides his fear under his lame attempts at humor.
JD	We all do.

(A beat.)

Narrator	How would you describe this place to someone who has never stepped foot?

(All searching. It's a complicated answer.)

Thomas	It's complicated.
JD	Right now…yeah, it's complicated. *(Celia smiles at JD.)*
Narr	Well, what's your…connection to this place? *(Searching for the right words. It's delicate.)* Your history…maybe in spite of, and maybe because of, its, your…current situation.

(No response. They are hesitant. Narrator jots down something in her pocket notebook.)

C'mon. It's ok. Give me something.

Sonya	*(Honestly.)* You won't find better people.
Saranda	Yep.
Sonya	Prouder.
Saranda	To a fault sometimes.
Dru	Most of the time.
Chad	*(Joking.)* Or people who know how to party better.

LeDeux   Fuck yeah!

(The group laughs.)

Renee   *(To LeDeux.)* Please grow up.

Narrator   Do you find it interesting that I mention the place first and you all go first to people?

Tricia   Can't talk about The Bayou without talking about people.

Ronnie   True.

Jackie   *(Joking.)* It's the Sportsman's Paradise, bitches.

Ronnie   That's such a crock of shit.

Jackie   Pelican license plate fucking paradise.

Ronnie   Stop cussing. It's disrespectful.

Jackie   *(Sincerely.)* Sorry.

Narr   No, it's fine actually.

Tricia   It's more than the freakin' "Sportsman's Paradise."

Saranda   The wetlands are like… *(Can't find the words.)* Like, I don't know… Special. *(She realizes "special" was an awkward choice of words.)*

Chad   You're special.

Saranda   *(Smiling, but with a hint of "fuck off".)* Yeah.

Renee   They are special.

Roxanne   Yeah.

Tricia   Yeah…

Renee   People come down here and they drive by the refineries. They're hideous. They look like giant space stations. Last summer I drove over the bridge at night

	with a cousin of mine from St. Louis. He looked over and saw all the lights and was like, "What the bleep is that? It looks like a post-apocalyptic Oz, what the bleep is it?"
Chad	You should have said, "That's the gas for your car, a-hole."
JD	Nice.
Chad	It's true though.
Thoreau	Yep. We're the support people for this country.
Narr	Do you think the country knows that?
Chad	No, m'am.
Renee	*(Continuing her train of thought.)* Then they drive down here and see the strip. Fast food. Gas stations. It's awful. They think that's what we are. Trashy. People who go deeper will see how amazing it is. Swamps, cypress, live oaks. Spanish moss. The magnolias. I can't say this without sounding stupid cheesy, but it's like, really, full of mystery here. Yeah, cheesy…but The Bayou is so beautiful. You just have to look. Is that silly?
Roxanne	No. Perfect.
Thoreau	*(She hit it on the head.)* Bam! *(An imitation of Emeril Lagasse.)*
	(Laughs.)
Saranda	That's why people don't leave. You can sense that specialty. *(She's not great with words.)* Speci-ality? Specialness? I don't know, but they don't want to leave. Used to not want to, anyway. Now everyone wants to get the hell out. *(Beat.)* Our families have been here for, like…forever.

Ronnie	Made it ours.
Thomas	Made us too.
Renee	Exactly.

(A beat.)

Thoreau	Have you seen the cypress graveyard?
Narr	*Which* graveyard?
Thoreau	Cypress.
Tricia	You need to go. They're dead, but still standing there. Every time I go the water is higher. They're just like… waiting there for the wake to knock 'em down.
Sonya	I can relate.
Tice	Yep.
Jackie	We survivors, dog!
Ronnie	Dog? *(To Narrator.)* He thinks he's a rapper.
Jackie	I got skills baby. Mad skills. Watch this. Give me a beat.

(Someone gives him a beat-box rhythm. Another person does the "wicki wickis." He raps.)

Jackie	The professor be coming, talkin' to us, 'bout our land and the consequentious loss. I'll tell her that I leavin' but I got no place go, now let's go get a 40 at the *Kum* and Go! *(He emphasizes Kum.)*

(Group laughs.)

Renee	Oh my God, I'm so embarrassed.
Dru	*You* are? Let she who throws the first stone…
Renee	What's that supposed to mean? *I'm* a good girl.

Chad	*(With sexual implication.)* That's what I heard.
LeDeux	*(Implying a past relationship.)* I'll vouch for it.
Renee	Oh my God!! *(Turns to Narrator.)* Would it be rude if I hit him?
Narr	No. I think he earned it.
Jackie	*(Drawing attention back to himself.)* Wicki wicki wicki!
JD	*(To Narrator. Referring to Jackie.)* He found his Dad's Beastie Boys tape last year and we lost him.

(Laughs. Celia smiles at JD. They have a relationship blooming.)

Renee	*(To Jackie.)* And consequentious is not a word.
Narr	Actually, writers make up words all the time. Shakespeare did it.
Saranda	Did Shakespeare say bitches? And "A 40 at the Kum and Go"? That is such a horrible stereotype.
Jackie	*(Raps.)* I'm a stereotype, you a stereotype, they come in shapes and sizes, even Cajun white.
Dru	Ok. That's actually funny.
Jackie	*(Raps.)* Funny what I am, despite my Uncle Sam, he's takin' all my bucks and us he likes to f…

(The group breaks in before he gets out the word fuck. "No!" "Stop!" Etc. They laugh.)

Thomas	*(To Narrator.)* The Bayou is perhaps not best known for its rap…

(Group laughs.)

Ronnie   Can we be serious? This is serious! Finally someone
            gives a crap. Can we please be, like, normal? Good
            Lord.

Chad   *(Miming phone.)* "Yeah, I'd like a large order of
            normal." *(To Ronnie.)* Would you like shrimp on it?

Tice   Local or imported?

            (Group laughs. A beat.)

Ronnie   *(Laughing gently.)* That's totally not funny.

            (A beat. Michelle raises her hand. Narrator nods to her.)

Michelle   Can I say something?

Narr   Yeah. Of course.

Michelle   When your families have been through so much crap,
            like most of ours, it… *(Searching.)*

Ronnie   Your history means a lot more.

Narr   Okay. I'm getting it. Tell me more.

Thoreau   Okay. Look at the Native Americans. *(Noting JD.)*
            They were so connected to their land that when it was
            taken away they sort of lost themselves, right? They
            struggled to retain their identity.

Roxanne   Do you have any idea what the hell you're talking
            about?

Thoreau   Yes, actually. Try picking up a book sometime. The
            Native Ameri-

JD   *(Cutting him off.)* Umm…hello. *(Sarcastically offers
            a cliché American Indian hello.)* "How!"

            (Some group laughs. Celia smiles at JD.)

Thoreau	…are *still* struggling. And why? Because people wanted gold? Oil? The Native Americans wanted success. They just looked at it differently, and they knew it meant respecting their environment. But, because they looked different, had different traditions, people labeled them savages, took their land-
Sonya	Slaughtered them.
Thoreau	But *they* fought back.
Ronnie	Yeah…that went well.
Thoreau	So are we, in our own way.
Narr	How so?
Thoreau	What people don't understand is that we're fighting for who we are, not just what we have. It's not just about losing land.
LeDeux	*(Overly enthusiastic.)* Bay-you through and through!!! *(A beat.)* Is that stupid?
Narr	*(Seriously.)* Yes. *(A beat. Ensemble laughs. She was joking.)*
LeDeux	Ha! Dr. Yankee making funny.
Narr	Yankee? Should I be offended by that?
Roxanne	No, it means he likes you.

(Laughs.)

LeDeux	Speaking of Yankees…
Roxanne	Please don't…
Son. & Sar.	Here we go.
LeDeux	One time I hooked up with this hot Brooklyn chick.
Renee	Oh God! Can you not?

LeDeux   Freaky hot. Even with that f-ed up accent. She was like, "So proud of New York." We took a subway into Times Square and she said that, "The City is like, one of the only places that if someone blindfolded you and dumped you in the middle of it you could take it off and know immediately where you were." I was like, "Holy crap, that's The Bayou." *(A beat. Sincerely.)* It's not like any other place. And neither are we. *(A beat. Turns to Renee.)* And did I say she was freaky hot?

Saranda   You're a pig. That was almost insightful.

Tice   Except in Louisiana you'd take off the blindfold and while your eyes were focusing you'd think, "Oh shii.., am I in Florida?" for a sec. *(Tice is handed a football as he crosses toward LeDeux.)* Then you'd see people under sixty and realize it wasn't Florida. You'd be like, "I think this is the Louisiana Bayou." Then you'd smell that gumbo and be like, "Yep, this is definitely Da Bayou, thank the Lord, praise Jesus, now get me some a dat gumbo!"

(Group laughs loudly. LeDeux jumps behind Tice like a football quarterback. The group cheers.)

LeDeux   *(He calls a play.)* Blue 42! Hike!

(Tice hikes the ball to LeDeux then runs across stage for a pass in a mock college football game. The ensemble roars like an SEC football crowd, yelling and cheering. LeDeux passes to Tice. The pass is complete. Both throw up their arms up in celebration. A winning touchdown. The crowd cheers. Tice and LeDeux celebrate, jump and bump chests, then fall into the arms of the screaming crowd, many of whom fall to the floor. The improvisational football play turns into laughter from the ensemble. A release. The Narrator steps gently forward. Sensing her presence, the laughter quiets. Then, an awkward pause.)

Narr   Don't stop having fun on my behalf.

(Silence. The Narrator takes notice that Michelle has something on her mind.)

Narr   Something you want to say?

Michelle   Yeah. *(Raises hand.)* Can I?

Narr   Please.

Michelle   This…this is our… *(She doesn't know how to say it.)*

Sonya   I don't think people can imagine what it's like to grow up in a place that you know is disappearing.

(A beat.)

Narr   *(A pivotal realization.)* I agree. You hurting?

Sonya   *(Respectfully. All are caught off guard emotionally.)* Yeah. We all are.

(A beat. Narrator leaves it alone.)

Ronnie   Somebody was talking about history. Our families have been tested. Together. Everybody here is really different, and God knows we fight, right? But I mean, we're black, we're white, Asian, Native American, German, Cajun, Hispanic, Creole, Mulatto, whatever. We still depend on each other. That's why we're so stubborn. Right? *(To others.)* Right?! When you've been tested togeth-

Sonya   We're still being tested.

Saranda   *(Sarcastic.)* Just in new and very inventive ways.

Ronnie   Yeah. But isn't that supposed to be like the American success story? All the struggles give you that patriotic bond or whatever? *(Shedding some humor on it.)* Now, multiply that feeling times a million, boil it some crawfish-

Dru	Play it some Zydeco.
Michelle	Family.
Sonya	Buy it some totally worthless waterfront property-
Son & Ron	And you've got The Bayou!
LeDeux	Um, you forgot baseball! This place is the freakin' baseball capital. You know how many professional football and baseball players come out of here? The NFL and the Majors should get together and build a giant zillion dollar barrier island to protect this resource. *(Meaning himself. Flexes.)*
Thomas	*(Sincerely.)* We do give our resources. But no one on the outside gives back.
Chad	Like now?
Narr	The *outside*?
Thomas	Yeah. It's hard to explain. You know there's more money spent on snow removal in Chicago every year than in wetland reconstruction for our entire state? My dad always says the anchor of our cultures is the estuary. "When it's dead, we're dead." It makes people angry, so yes, sometimes it feels like us against them. This is our home. I don't know anyone who would want to leave their God-given home because of something someone else did. Would you?
Narr	No.
Dru	We did it too. Take some fucking blame.
Thomas	My *point* is…the people here *are* special, but so is the place. You can't separate the two.
Sonya	The Bayou is our community. It sounds heady-like… but…it defines us.

Jackie   *(Making fun of her choice of words.)* It sounds
            "heady-like?"

Roxanne   *(To Jackie.)* Please shut up.

Sonya   It does.

Narr   And have the people defined the land?

JD   Yes…for better and worse.

            (Celia watches JD. An irony in his statement.)

Narr   *(Takes note.)* For better and worse…

            *(A loud hurricane siren stops them. An official sounding
            PSA voice-over begins. The ensemble has heard this a
            hundred times. It's nothing new. They change to time-killing
            mode; chewing nails, brushing hair, etc. The Narrator is
            both confused and intrigued by the PSA, as well as by the
            non-reaction the students have to the announcement.)*

Voice-Over Hurricane Education Alert. Hurricanes are the
            products of the tropical ocean and atmosphere.
            Powered by heat from the sea, they are steered by
            the easterly trade winds and the temperate westerly's
            as well as by their own ferocious energy. Landfall is
            the term used to indicate the moment a hurricane hits
            land. Over the past several years, the warning systems
            have provided adequate time for people on coastland
            communities to move inland when hurricanes
            threaten. Please note: the warning system may be void
            if you can't travel because you are elderly, disabled, a
            beloved family pet, or too damn poor to afford a full
            tank of gas and a motel. Thank you.

            *(Narrator looks to others for an explanation. It doesn't
            come.)*

JD   *(To Narrator.)* You get used to it.

            (A beat. Narrator refers to her notes.)

Narr   A question. How many of your grandparents grew up here?

(All hands up except for Thoreau.)

Narr   How many of your parents?

(Same hands rise.)

Narr   How many of you are going to raise your families here?

(Only Saranda's hand goes up. This is the first time some have noted this about each other.)

(A loud school bell erupts. The group moves loudly to seated spaces on the floor, facing US, and erupts into a classroom paper fight, throwing wads of paper and generally acting as if the teacher has just left the classroom and they've gone out of control.)

Ensemble   *(General Improvisation.)* Whooooh! You missed. Ouch. Missed again. Your mama missed. Is that as hard as you can throw? Etc.

(Tice stands US of the group to make a report. He is suddenly victim to a barrage of paper wad attacks.)

Tice   This is my Political Science report on leadership.

(Ensemble reacts. "Boo. Sit down," etc.)

            Boo all you want. I agree. *(A beat.)* Frankly, I'm pissed...

(Ensemble reacts again, hitting him with some paper wads.)

            I've been given this assignment on political leadership, and I don't want to be disrespectful, but I think it's a joke.

(The ensemble continues to react as he begins, but as they hear more of his report they begin to relate and become

consumed by his words. They gradually become quiet, and, by the end, frozen in silence.)

But, I'm living in a system where grades matter, and if I want to do something with my life, I need the grades. So here it is. My report on leadership. *(He moves between reading and speaking freely.)* I think our political leadership is f-ed. Sorry. Like I said, I'm upset. I think it's necessary for a society to have leaders that maintain the will of the people. To have political leaders with morals, and who place their own needs behind the needs of the citizens. Especially citizens who are hurting…who lost their jobs and can't afford food for their family…ones who lost their insurance and can't fix the hole in their roof. Who are the insurance companies paying off, I wonder? Leadership. Citizens who live next to a refinery and can't afford the gas to drive to school. Yeah. Political leadership. I know it's important, but I'm not sure I can even tell you what it is, or that I've seen it. Where *are* our political leaders? I hear about them and see them on the news but they never seem to talk about us. They don't seem to have any idea of what is going on in their own basement. Their basement is filling up with water and I'm in it. It's bullshit. *(A beat.)* My family…my family is awesome. But I have to go home from school every day and watch my dad disintegrate from working for a company that is helping to destroy the things that he loves. He doesn't have a choice if we wanna eat. Dad is the greatest man alive, and he hates himself. Where is the leadership? I go to a school that might not be here in 10 years, or maybe even after the next hurricane, because our coastline is receding. I'm 17, words like receding and disintegrate shouldn't even be in my vocabulary. Where is the leadership? I look at my little sister knowing that she will never know how great our heritage is. Her world isn't even what my world was and I'm only six years older. I'm scared for her. I'm in high school, we aren't supposed to have to worry about stuff like this. That's for the leadership. But I love her more than anything, and nothing's getting better. Sometimes…I watch my grandmother cry when she thinks I'm not looking. She's proud. She's the anchor of our family. But we are disappearing. I'm disappearing. Where is the leadership? *(A beat.)* Sometimes when I get pissed I go outside to sit on the tire swing I've had since I was a kid, and then I remember that it's half underwater now. Leadership. I come to school and I look at my friends…and I know they're hurting just as much as I am, but I think if we actually talked about things, we'd explode. So we talk parties and sports and joke about how bad things are, about how good the fishing is gonna be from the roof of the Wal-Mart. *(A few people giggle.)* But it's not a joke! It's not! I'm scared for my friends. We're hurting. We're dying inside. Political leadership… *(A long beat.)* On my assignment sheet the last question was "What would you ask if you had the opportunity to sit down with a national politician?" *(A beat.)* I wouldn't yell at them. I would ask them to come to my house for dinner. Eat some gumbo. Shake my dad's dirty hand. I'd show them my tire swing. Maybe they'd listen to the jokes and see how much we're all hurting underneath. Then I'd introduce them to my grandma and say "See, now that's a leader."

(The ensemble is struck by his story, to which they all relate. They are silent. Frozen. Tice sits.)

Celia   *(Turns DS and begins reading what she written.)*
               Once upon a time…somewhere between yesterday
               and tomorrow, stands a village. Nestled in among the
               primeval swamps and majestic cypress, the village
               struggles for breath in a new world. Once bustling

with life and flourishing with the wealth of happy subsistence, the village now fights the encroaching water from the south.

(She crosses toward JD. He gently unfreezes and watches her.)

The trials of poverty and the yearly beatings of hurricanes are so frequent they now feel ritualistic to those hearty souls remaining there, absorbed into the identity of a people strong and willful. The village seems to float between two levees. One, a reminder of the historic past, and the other, a sign of a diminishing future. Once upon a time…the families here were farmers and shrimpers, living at one with the water that now encompasses their homes, threatens their very being. The children once waded in the marshes and played among the cypress that, now skeletal, stand half drowned on the water's horizon. Upon one of the cypress is a knife carving. Written in the hand of youth, it reads:

Celia & JD   *(He speaks with her.)* "Gabriel loves Evangeline."

(They smile at one another. This is their story she is writing.)

Celia   The wind-driven water slaps at the letters carved on the forlorn tree *(She sits next to JD.)* soaking the testament to youthful love that once stood six feet off the dry earth.

Narr   So what's the root problem here? With the wetlands? I've heard a lot of different perspectives, from politicians, community leaders, citizens, scientists… educators. Why do *you* think the wetlands are receding?

(Each unfreezes as he/she speaks.)

Dru   Fucking Army Corps.

JD   Oil industry.

Renee   Hurricanes don't help.

Jackie   Channelization of the Mississippi.

Thomas   Global Warming?

Ronnie   Big oil.

JD   Already said that.

Sonya   Crooked politicians.

Roxanne   Tanker wake.

Chad   The levees.

Tice   Dredging.

Michelle   The *money* industry.

LeDeux   The canals.

Saranda   Ignorance.

           (Celia stops writing. Looks up.)

Thoreau   D. All of the above.

           (A moment.)

Dru   *(Deadpan.)* Jesus hates us.

           (Others laugh. A beat.)

Narr   That's a lot of answers.

Sonya   That's the Cliff Notes.

Thomas   "There is a way that seems right to a man, but in the
              end it leads to death." Proverbs.

Thoreau	(*To Thomas.*) Yeah. (*To Narr.*) Look. It's complicated. It's all of those things. The Army Corps screwed up, the politicians had their hand in it. Comes down to the basic facts…we channelized the river, dredged and cut up the wetlands with canals. All that let the saltwater come in and kill the marshes. Now there's no natural barrier so the water just keeps encroaching.
Tricia	Encroaching. Good word.
Dru	And why? For oil. It's such bullshit.
Renee	It's not just the oil companies fault. We let them do it.
Dru	We had a choice?
Renee	Doesn't your dad work for oil?
Dru	Isn't your dad a politician?
Renee	My mom. What's your point?
Dru	What's yours?
Thoreau	Her point is that it's complicated. We can't look at the problems objectively because we're a part of them. It's environmental. It's political. It's social. It's all of it. The causes are obvious, it's the solutions… it's getting people to take responsibility- which isn't happening, getting it paid for- which isn't happening, and getting the government to help fix it- which definitely isn't happening. Honestly, I think the only thing left is to un-channelize the river and get the hell out.
Michelle	That's not gonna happen either.
Thoreau	It could.
Michelle	Yeah, and millions of people can just up and move. Sure, who's gonna pay for that? My parents would rather die than move.

Chad	They might.
Roxanne	*(To Chad, sternly.)* Nice.
Narr	So what, then?
Tricia	They're putting sediment back on the marshes.
Thoreau	They?
Saranda	And what happens to the fishing industry? What if *your* family fishes that part of the Gulf?
Tricia	…rebuild the barrier islands.
LeDeux	Ok, I'll pay for it when I'm rich. Want some money? Here you go. Some for you. Some for you…

(LeDeux walks through the group and pretends to hand out money. Others scramble for it, playing along. Improv. A playful ruckus.)

Tricia	*(Frustrated, she vocally intervenes on the improv.)* We make the people who did it pay for it. If they did it, the oil companies need to close the canals and fix the wetlands.
LeDeux	Hey! *(Joking.)* And the Corps can do the engineering.
JD	*(Tired of avoiding the issue with teenage play and jokes.)* You're all missing the point, that we are part of the problem! We're living here and most of us have family that works for oil. We keep saying one thing and doing another. I'm guilty. It doesn't make any sense. I mean, if we really mean it, we won't work for them.
Dru	I don't.
Saranda	*(Slightly offended.)* Sure, because there's so many other options.
LeDeux	*(Avoiding the argument.)* Baseball freaking capital.

JD   Also. It's not just oil. It's bigger than that. I mean, it's obvious what's happening here, and nothing ever gets solved by politicians.

Renee   That's not fair.

JD   But it's true, right? So if we can't depend on our state politicians, when is the federal government gonna help? When we cut off their oil? Do you know what would happen to this country if the refineries-

Jackie   Let's blow up the pipeline! *(Jumps up.)*

LeDeux   Yeah!

Jackie   Fuck yeah, bitches! Kaboom!!!

            (Cheers.)

Tice   Yeah but then we'd be screwed too.

Jackie   Damn. *(Sits.)*

            (A beat.)

Saranda   A hurricane will do it anyway.

            (A long beat.)

JD   The point is, we can't depend on anybody but ourselves. So what do we do? We all sit around and complain. Pretty soon we'll be complaining under water.

            (Celia takes note. A beat.)

Ronnie   *(To Narrator. Explaining the frustrations of the group.)* Everybody has an opinion. It *is* really complicated. We're in a no-win.

Narr   And?

Ronnie   *(To others.)* We need to start fixing stuff ourselves.

Chad	*(Sarcastic.)* Sure. Okay.
Narr	*(To Ronnie.)* How?
Roxanne	Better communication.
Tricia	Yep.
Chad	What?
Roxanne	Communication.
Chad	*(Joking.)* What?
Roxanne	*(Getting the joke.)* Comm-un-iii-caaayyy-shyuun!
Thoreau	It's unsustainable. Something's gonna give.
Chad	*(Feigning tears.)* In the meantime lives are being wrecked and I have to go to school with these ignorant assholes.
Renee	*(Sarcastic.)* That's really funny. God! This is serious.
LeDeux	Oh please. Go call your politician Mommy.
Renee	I will. And you can go back to your Daddy's shrimp shack!
Ronnie	Stop it, you guys!
Tice	Let 'em argue. *(Aside to others.)* Sexual tension.
Renee	Screw you!
Tice	Really? Okay.
LeDeux	Are you on the rag?
Renee	Shut up!
LeDeux	*(Mocking her.)* Shut up.
Renee	Shut the hell up!

Jackie	Damn, girl means bidness.
Roxanne	*(To Jackie.)* Don't be an idiot.
Jackie	Was I talking to you?
Michelle	Here we go.
Jackie	*(To Michelle.)* Go sell some fruit.
Michelle	What?
Dru & Sar	Leave her alone.
Jackie	Screw you both.
Chad	I already did.
Ronnie	You are such a jerk!

(The conversation takes a vicious turn. The students erupt into an all-out improvisational vocal battle with comments that become very personal, encroaching upon family, economic status, and race. They argue throughout the space. Just as it could become physical it is interrupted by a loud siren. They freeze in tableau, except Celia, who keeps writing. Another PSA voice-over begins. The Narrator takes notes.)

Voice-Over Hurricane Education Alert. One of the most important tasks you will face will be preparing your child for a hurricane disaster. This should be done in a non-threatening way. Try to be positive. Remind your children that many of the things they care about may be lost forever, and emphasize that, over time, material things can be replaced, as long as you have the money or the insurance to replace them. If you do not, or if your insurance company hits the road, good luck. Your children will be angry and bitter and are likely to become a teen pregnancy statistic or victim of juvenile drug addiction. Have a wonderful day.

Celia   *(Reading what she has written.)* Some years ago, a
           shrimper named Benedict lived in the village with his
           beautiful daughter Evangeline. From a long Cajun
           lineage, Benedict was his father's only son, and
           Evangeline was Benedict's only child. She carried
           the unspoken weight of cultural tradition upon her
           shoulders.

        (JD unfreezes and turns to her.)

           She was yet a teenager, but had a soul far older than
           her earthbound years. Her eyes were dark as the
           night swamp. Soft brown hair kissed her cheeks and
           traveled downward where it hugged shoulders that
           drew resemblance to her deceased mother and her
           mother before her. Evangeline's heart belonged to
           Gabriel, her childhood friend. *(JD sits next to her.
           She is now reading to and about him.)* Gabriel was
           the son of an Indian tribal leader. He was a handsome
           and honest young man who inspired hope in others
           with the ease of a floating gull. *(Thinks, looks at JD,
           then writes.)* It was once said that he held a glint
           of heavenly serenity in his eyes. Like Evangeline,
           Gabriel was an only child, and he took certain pride in
           maintaining the culture and traditions of his heritage.

        (Celia and JD hold hands. A beat.)

Narr   *(To the group.)* How has your family been impacted
           by the wetlands loss?

        *(Each individual breaks freeze and turns DS as they speak.
        During the following monologues, the Narrator walks
        through and among the group, taking notes, observing them
        from the "outside." They continue to speak DS as if she
        were in front of them. After speaking, each actor remains
        unfrozen and listens to the others from the group.)*

Saranda   My God. I don't even know where to start. My
           grandparents used to farm and raise some livestock.

They did pretty well, Almost everything is oil now. Even that's being "farmed" out, they have all these people coming in for those jobs. I don't know, I guess it's cheaper. If you look in town you'll see these really big brick houses that are really nice and right next to them will be some little rancher with a tarp on the roof. Well, we're one of the ranchers and the oil execs are the big brick ones. My dad did a lot of stuff. He worked rigs…he worked on some shrimp boats. He's dead. That sounds so dramatic. *(As Scarlett O'Hara.)* He's dead! *(As self.)* I'm ok with it. It was a long time ago. *(She's not ok with it.)* So my mom helps me take care of Aiden while I'm in school. His daddy's on a rig. Did you see Aiden's picture? *(Showing it).* He's not even three and he already knows his letters. I swear to God! He's so smart. Don't get me started cuz I won't stop. And he's such the little ladies man. He calls everybody "sweetie." It's so cute. I'm talking to some lady in the checkout line and he looks at her and is like, "Hi sweetie." It's the cutest thing ever. But really, don't let me get started. *(She playfully hugs his pic.)*

Narr   And his future?

Saranda   Aiden? Oh God… *(Caught off guard.)* Who knows? I would love him to grow up here. I guess…I'm just hoping we're still here next year. I love it here. *(Thinks.)* Ok, maybe a football player…

Michelle   I work in my family's grocery. I know, I know, it's such a cliché. My great-grandfather opened the store and we've had it since. Most of my family works there. Another cliché. It's nice, I guess. It is hard though. We never have enough money. We used to be able to sell cheap produce and seafood- but with shortages we have to try to make money on other stuff. Oh my God, it almost killed my dad to have to get a liquor license. Killed him. He was like, "This is not what my grandfather wanted for this family. This is not the values that he worked for." Every time he sells somebody a six-pack he looks like he's going to kill them. I actually feel bad for the people buying it. It hurts him a lot. Anyway, I really want to go to NYU and study business. I have the grades, but…I don't know. My grandfather is really sick too, and…I don't know, I just don't know what would happen to my family if I left.

Thoreau   My Dad's a hurricane researcher up at the university. My mom teaches third grade science. So, we wouldn't even be here if the wetlands were ok. I like it here. I love it actually. I don't know how I'd feel if I completely grew up here though. Pissed off I guess. It's all pretty f-ed up.

JD   So, I'm Houma Indian. *(Celia watches him.)* That's not normally the first thing I tell people, but… we spent hundreds of years living sustainably. Sustainable is the new cool word but we did it for a long time. You have to live a floodable lifestyle. Houma would move with the seasons…and the hurricanes. There's no predictability and no buffer anymore though, you couldn't do that if you wanted to. But the problem is not that there are more hurricanes, it's that there are no wetlands left to protect us when they come. My family has been hit pretty hard. Most of us work in oil now. I've done it in summers. It kills me though, because I know what's caused all this, so to work for the industry that has hurt your way of life…it's crazy. It eats at us, even if we don't say it out loud. I feel like Judas. *(Beat.)* I don't know what else we're supposed to do though.

Narr   What would you like to do?

JD   Something. Anything. We've worked hard to help, to
          fix things. I...I think my family is giving up though.
          I can feel it. Everybody's always talking about
          heritage. "Heritage." It's kind of a joke. It's falling
          apart. There is this weight. Especially on us...the kids.
          Nobody says it, but it feels like everybody is looking
          to us to fix stuff, to save generations of tradition.
          Houma tradition. Heritage. It's a lot of responsibility.
          (Beat.) I want to do what I can. I'll do ...everything I
          can, but I do...I think my family is finally giving up.
          I don't know what will happen. *(An afterthought.)*
          Yeah...Judas.

Renee   My family is doing fine. I mean, we're always doing
          stuff- meetings, public events, whatever...my mom
          is a politician, so we're always doing things for the
          wetlands. Our family loves it here, and we know how
          bad it is. It's really bad. The thing is though, some of
          the people here have to help themselves. Everyone
          is so negative. I guess its poverty. But, I mean, if
          you screw the insurance company because you're
          broke, of course they're gonna split, and guess what,
          you'll be more broke. It's a horrible cycle. How can
          people expect politicians to help if people won't help
          themselves? It doesn't make any sense. I feel bad
          saying that. I don't know. I guess people do what they
          have to do. We are scared though...my family. My
          mom is always smiling and shaking hands and trying
          to promote the wetlands, but she gets home and loses
          it sometimes. *(A beat.)* Whatever. She's scared. We
          all are. My family...it's like we have to lead this
          double life. All smiles on the outside. Inside we're
          just as scared as everybody else.

Thomas   Let me read you something. *(Quotes from a Mass
          program.)* "God of all power. At your command all
          things came to be; the vast expanse of interstellar
          space, galaxies, suns, the planets in their courses,

and this fragile earth, our island home. By your will they were created and have their being. From the primal elements you brought forth the human race, and blessed us with memory, reason, and skill. You made us the rulers of creation. But we turned against you and betrayed your trust, and turned against one another. Have mercy Lord, for we are sinners in your sight." The wetland problems are man-made. Man-made! But God is still watching. Human beings are the only animal that has the capacity to change. That's God's will. God has always taken our hands and walked us to the right path. This is not all for nothing. It's gotta be in his plan. Look at us. There is still hope, and that's God. My mother always says that when you still have hope, God puts a little glimmer in your eye. My faith tells me He will guide us. I believe that. My family believes that. We struggle, but we have certainty through our faith. He will guide us. I really believe that. I have… *(A beat.)* I have to.

Dru   Honestly, my family can go fuck themselves. My Dad is like Mr. Oil. Seriously. They don't get it. You cannot possibly live in a system that's chewing off its own foot and expect to last very long. They just can't look outside of their little fucking box to realize that we *are* the problem. How can you destroy the wetlands one day and go fishing the next? It's fucked up. They're totally clueless.

Narr   Does that bother you?

Dru   I'm over it. They're way too fucking gone. *(Beat.)* I lied. It bothers me. It bothers me a lot. *(A beat.)* Whatever.

(A Beat.)

LeDeux *(Joking.)* Did I mention I play baseball? *(Flexes like the Hulk.)* Argggh. No juice needed for this gun, Mr.

McGwire. *(Flexes right arm.)* No HGH in this gun,
Mr. Bonds. *(Flexes left.)* Bam! *(Mimes home run.)*
Rahhhhhh! *(Fans cheering.)* Okay, focus…focus. I'm
ready. Start with?

Narr   Your name means "the second." What's your dad do?

LeDeux   My dad?

Narr   Yes.

LeDeux   My dad…played Minor League. Said the timing just
didn't work out for him to get to the Majors. I think
I may have been that "bad timing" actually. He's in
construction. He's done, oh, let me see… oil, shrimp,
gator tours. We do okay though. It's hard sometimes I
guess.

Narr   How so?

LeDeux   Everyone's affected by what's going on. You can't
not be. *(A long beat.)* I was playing a game last
week and, and…my mind was way out of it. I'm
daydreaming of big boobies or something and I let a
ball slide by that I should have grabbed no problem.
An LSU guy was there so the timing…it really
blew. We get in the car and my dad freaks. "Fucking
fucking fucking fuck fuck! How could you fuck fuck?
Don't you know how much this fucking fucking fuck
means? What the fuck? Fuck!" He never cusses.
Ever. I think he just reacted. He just wants me to get
the hell out of here so bad. Also, everybody here is
carrying a huge weight all the time. Everybody. It's
just hard. I mean…things are really freaking hard and
who knows where we'll even be next year, right? My
dad doesn't show emotion normally so I think it just
built up and he took it out on me.

Tricia   *(Holding guitar.)* My family…is…normal. We're
dealing with the same stuff everybody else is.

My dad is a mechanic and my mom is a guidance counselor. *She* hears some stuff, that's for sure. She's always talking about the teen suicide rate. People are a lot worse than we are. *(A beat.)* I mean, people have totally lost their houses, their jobs, their insurance…died. It's stupid what's happening. When people struggle their families get ripped up. Bad crap happens. It's getting worse. So, my mom is an annoying communication freak. She sees all this bad stuff at work and she's like, "If we keep communicating as a family we can overcome anything." That's true, I guess, but communication is a lot easier when you have a job or you're like, not knocked up at 15. *(Thinks of Saranda.)* Sorry, I'm not downing anybody. Really. My family is okay. We're okay. But we also know that we're gonna have to move. Yep. Everybody knows it. I'm just tired of evacuating like every ten minutes. It's awful. Even if you have "communication." It wears on you. God it's awful. It does give me time to write though. *(An ironic laugh.)* Ooh. Wanna hear something?

(She sings/plays the song she's working on. "Someday.")

> It's kinda late,
> but I'm not sleeping.
> A million thoughts in my head,
> keep me awake
> as I lay seeking,
> the key to my piece of mind.
> My fame my glory,
> written like a bedtime story,
> with an ending that is happy every time... *(Beat.)*

It's not done yet. *(She freezes.)*

Narr *(Honestly.)* That's beauti-

(Interjecting over the Narrator, Sonya unfreezes and begins to argue with her mother, who is unseen. After Sonya, others follow suit one by one. Each character's dialogue below overlaps the final few words of the character prior.)

Sonya   Mom. Listen for a sec. Listen! I'm not going. There is no way we can afford that. There is no way. I know. I know. You think I don't want to go!? But how is that supposed to happen? With everything we're dealing with, there is no way I'm gonna jump into a nursing program and pretend everybody else isn't suffering for it to happen. It's not gonna happen! *(She freezes.)*

Roxanne   *(Unfreezes.)* Pleaaaase. Dad. I'm not being selfish. I swear. It's one week. One week. I promise I'll pay you back. It's New York. It's Broadway. Pleease. You have nooo idea how much this would mean to me. I promise. I'll pay you back. Daaaddddyyy. *(Freeze.)*

Tice   *(Unfreezes.)* I have to get a freaking computer, Dad. How am I supposed to do my photos if I don't have a computer? No. Everything is digital. Everything. If I want to do anything with my life I've gotta at least have the basics, and for me it's just a cheap computer! Why are we even arguing? I don't get it. Are we that broke? *(Freeze.)*

Dru   *(Unfreezes.)* Are you kidding me? There's no way, Dad. There's no way I'm going to that. I'm not gonna sit around and act all "picnicy" with a bunch of tycoon a-holes. Yeah, we can all sit around and eat little corporate oil wieners and talk about our money and the evils of liberalism. It makes me sick. There is no way I'm going to that. No way. *(Freeze.)*

Chad   *(Unfreezes.)* I already enlisted! OK. I'm sorry. I am. Actually, no I'm not. No, you're right, I didn't ask you. I'm sorry. I knew you'd say no, so why would I? Why would I? Dad did it. Granddad did it. Why can't

I serve my country? If I serve and get killed at least I did it doing something. What's my other option, stick around here and work at Wal-Mart for the rest of my life? That's not a choice. It's not an option, Mom! I'm doing this. I have to! *(Freeze.)*

Ronnie   *(Unfreezes.)* No, I am not "consuming alcohol." And who even calls it that? I don't know why he told you that. I have no idea. That's just stupid. That's the most stupid thing I ever heard. And even if I did, no one has any right to say anything. I study my butt off. When's the last time I got a B? Exactly! Never! Why couldn't I have a little fun if I wanted to for once? God knows you did. God, I have to be perfect at everything! *(Freeze.)*

Jackie   *(Unfreezes.)* Yes. I did. Suspended. Two weeks. I don't care what he said, I didn't start it. I swear to God. I was walking down the hall and he just punched me. I have no idea why. I didn't "stab" him. He's a liar. I hit him back, I had a pencil in my hand, and it scratched his face. It was an accident. Did anybody ask him why he hit me? Did they? This is such bullshit! I'm so sick of this! *(Freeze.)*

(The ensemble layers in, one by one, unfreezing and erupting into argumentative dialogue with an imaginary parent, moving slowly DS into a line as they fight. Celia does not fight. She writes and moves US. The volume and intensity rises with each additional voice. Narrator observes.)

Thoreau   *(Argues with parents!)*

LeDeux   *(Argues with parents!)*

Saranda   *(Argues with parents!)*

Michelle   *(Argues with parents!)*

JD	*(Argues with parents!)*
Thomas	*(Argues with parents!)*
Renee	*(Argues with parents!)*
Tricia	*(Argues with parents!)*

(The others, who have already argued, also unfreeze and layer into the parental arguments.)

(A loud siren. The ensemble, now in a line DS, sit slowly in resignation. They await the PSA. Nothing comes. Uncertainty. The lack of a PSA following the siren holds meaning to them. A long beat. They enter a soft freeze, except for Dru, Celia, and JD. Dru begins writing down and plucking out some music on the piano. It's the beginning of the song "Through it All." JD watches Celia speak.)

Celia   *(Still working on her story.)* Gabriel and Evangeline's childhood friendship grew into love, and at the age of 18 they found themselves preparing for their wedding. In the unseen horizon, an approaching hurricane silently bristled and grew in power. Their families gathered at Benedict's house for a party celebrating the engagement. It was the eve of their wedding. On that hot August day, the two families danced and ate and passed on old stories under the shade of the live oaks. The joyous celebration painted two beautiful portraits, one of young love, and another of the coming together of two cultures…

(JD listens. She looks at him.)

…of two cultures proud, colorful, and resourceful. To their families, the bond of Evangeline and Gabriel also marked the survival of cultural lineage and long held-family traditions. Their love planted a new seed of hope in the village.

(Frustrated with what she is writing, Dru pounds the piano.)

Dru   Fuck.

(A loud siren. This time followed by a PSA. Dru and Celia listen acutely. Others listen but are more resigned, emotionally exhausted.)

Voice-Over   Hurricane Education Alert. Your 10 Step Guide to Hurricane Survival. Step 1. Decide where you will go. Step 2. Learn the evacuation routes and procedures. Step 3. The survival kit.

(Narrator takes notes.)

Dru   What the fuck is that? *(To Celia.)* Do you have a survival kit?

(Celia does not reply.)

Voice-Over   Step 4. Preparing for special needs family members, children, elderly, disabled. Step 5. Provision for animals. Step 6. Preparing important documents and memorabilia. Step 7. Insurance and property inventory. Step 8. Protecting your home and property. Step 9. Plan for family notification and communication. Step 10. Financial Planning. Most people assume "nothing bad will happen" or "we had a bad one last year." In Louisiana a disaster is declared every 1.1 years. The disaster supply kit includes your supplies such as water, food, first aid, clothing, bedding, tools, emergency supplies, and special needs items. You should anticipate spending $500 or more on items you don't have. *(The VO begins to speed up and becomes more frenzied. Dru tries to take it in.)* A home of 1,400 square feet with 11 to 13 openings requiring 5/8" plywood, visqueen, screws, and duct tape will cost another $600. *(Speeds up more.)* Cost of evacuating out of the risk area will include fuel expenses, eating in restaurants, and staying in hotels if you can locate one. If you require medical attention add to your budget the cost for 2 months supply. *(Dru can't take it in.)* You must also plan for a decrease in earnings revenue-

Dru   Shut up.

Voice-Over   *(Now so fast it's almost unintelligible, like Alvin and the Chipmunks but faster.)* The Office of Homeland Security is responsible for the coordination of those actions needed to protect the lives and property of its residents when threatened from natural disasters as well as man-made occurrences such as-

Dru   *(Yells.)* Shut up!

(Silence. It stopped. Overwhelmed, Dru leaves stage.)

Celia   …a new seed of hope in the village. *(Thinks. Goes back to writing.)*

(A beat.)

Narr   *(To group.)* How are you doing? I mean really? Really doing?

(Seated in the line, each member of the ensemble resides in their own emotional space, deflated, responding but detached. JD has joined them. They do not look at each other as they respond.)

Sonya   Thank you.

Narr   For what?

Sonya   For asking. Nobody asks.

Narr   Why do you think that is?

Tice   Afraid of the answer.

Chad   *(To self.)* They should be.

Renee	No they shouldn't.
Thoreau	Too consumed with their own problems.
Chad	This will be their problem.
Thomas	Too busy looking at the "bigger" issues.
Saranda	Insurance crisis.
JD	Money, re-building.
Ronnie	We get lost in it all.
Renee	We do.
Tricia	Hide how we feel.
Michelle	It's just the way things are.
Ronnie	Yeah, but we're running out of time.
Jackie	Why ask? The answer sucks.
JD	When something's part of who you are, nobody thinks to ask how it's affecting you. It's just who you are. Period.

(Celia silently agrees.)

Saranda	We deal with it.
Narr	How? *(Silence.)* How do you deal with it? *(Silence. A beat.)* How do you deal with it?

(Silence. Long beat. No comment.)

Jackie	Wanna hear my new rap?
Sonya	No.
Jackie	Damn. Harsh.

(An awkward beat.)

LeDeux   Did I tell you this is the baseball capital of the world?

Roxanne   Of the world now? Impressive.

Narr   Why is that question so hard to answer?

    (A beat.)

Michelle   We… *(No words.)*

Ronnie   Say it.

    (Michelle says nothing. A beat.)

Ronnie   We're doing. That's all we can do.

    (All except Celia enter a soft freeze. The Narrator continues to observe.)

Celia   *(Reading what she has written, she travels DS behind the line.)* The engagement celebration was interrupted by the sound of loud church bells. The desperate frequency of the bells marked the imminent arrival of a hurricane that had grown extremely dangerous, threatening to lay waste to their lives. Not yet married, the responsibilities of Evangeline and Gabriel first lay with their families. *(Behind JD, she places a hand on his shoulder. He reaches up and holds it.)* The lovers shared a kiss, then parted ways and went with their families to prepare for the storm. Comforted by their unbreakable bond, Evangeline and Gabriel's kiss was certain as night.

          As the storm approached, it became clear to the residents of this village that an unlikely future lay before all who remained. With communication impossible, Gabriel and Evangeline were left no choice but to flee with their families and trust that they would be together soon. Gabriel's desperate attempt to reach Evangeline before departing was interrupted by vigilant parents who feared for the life of their son. Evangeline also protested her departure without Gabriel, but followed the trustful wisdom of her father and began to travel north.

And the hurri-

(A siren interrupts. This one feels different. Louder. More shrill. Another PSA.)

Voice-Over Please evacuate the region. I repeat, please evacuate the region. A mandatory evacuation order is in effect. A category five hurricane is approaching. If you choose to remain authorities cannot account for your safety. I repeat, authorities cannot account for your safety. A mandatory evacuation is in effect. Authorities cannot account for your safety.

(Deflated, emotionally exhausted, the ensemble slowly begins to depart the stage. During their exit crosses, each engages in the reverse trajectory of their entrance in blackout from the top of Act I, exiting where they entered and utilizing the same dialogue, except this time they are visible to the audience. The physicality underscoring individual dialogue should feel like sharp violent interruptions to their melancholy departures. DS, in the midst of the exits, JD and Celia share a hard embrace, then a kiss. JD departs. The Narrator departs unnoticed amidst the ruckus. Tricia and Celia remain onstage and do not participate in the ensemble exit dialogue.)

Ensemble   We're in here!
Please God!
Get inside!
My God.
It's a baby.
I'm afraid.
Get in the attic!
Where's the dog!
I'm not going without the fucking dog!

I'm so thirsty!
You're hurting me.
Get in the fucking car!
No!
Hurry up!
We're out of gas!
Leave it!
God help us.
Get in the car now!
The phone is dead!
The road is blocked.
There's no gas.
Where's grandma?
Daddy!!
Help!
Etc, etc!

(Tricia is now alone onstage with Celia. She plays guitar and sings.)

Tricia   *(From Saints.)* …all my folks have gone before me, all my friends and all my kin…

(Stops playing. Sings a capella from Someday.)

    …the key to my piece of mind,
    my fame, my glory,
    written like a bedtime story,
    with an ending that is… *(A beat.)*

(Tricia leaves. Celia quietly reads what she has just written.)

Celia   …they began to travel north. *(A beat.)*
    And the hurricane devastated the village.

(Blackout. End of Act I.)

Act II

(In blackout, the sound of a loud hurricane pervades the house. The sound grows so deep the house trembles. After some time, it slowly fades. Silence in the darkness. Lights gently up. The Narrator enters.)

Narrator   Act II. Ten months later. Post-hurricane. *(She observes the forthcoming action.)*

(Lights fully rise to find the actors upstage in the same tableau as the beginning of Act I. One character is noticeably missing. JD. A special brings attention to his absence. The ensemble takes solemn notice.)

Celia   The village was devastated. Weeks later, when residents began to trickle back, they encountered the aftermath. Many of those who could not flee had perished, and waste was laid to the community and its surrounding farms. What the hurricane winds had not destroyed from above, the flood waters suffocated from below. Many homes were washed away, drowned forever by the encroaching southern waters. Among them was the home of Gabriel. The people of the village, including Gabriel, who had lost their homes and livelihoods, found themselves scattering to distant regions, left with no choice but to leave the place of their heritage and take root elsewhere. With the community and its resources damaged, Evangeline and Gabriel's desperate attempts to reach each other were met with continued frustration. Weeks later, Evangeline and her family returned to the village, where she turned her full energy to searching for signs of Gabriel. Guided by the strength of hope only present in young lovers, she often found herself under the cypress where she and Gabriel had once professed their undying love…the cypress where he had once carved "Gabriel Loves Evangeline."

(Celia watches as JD special slowly fades. A magnolia flower falls to the stage from above where JD would have been standing.)

> …the cypress where they had promised to meet should life ever part them.

(Tricia and Dru are working on a song, "Through it All." Piano with leading chords only. During the song, the rest of the ensemble moves from the US tableaus to spaces throughout the stage. They transition methodically, an indication of the emotional journey through which they have traveled. As they move, they quietly mutter their lines that opened and closed Act I.)

Tricia & Dru   I hope to find you…

(Finding key, etc. Re-working.)

> I hope to find you
> on a snowy winter morn,
> laughing beside me…

(They stop. Re-work.)

> on a snowy winter morn,
> laughing beside me,
> on a bed that's soft and warm.
> And as the days pass…

(They stop. Re-work.)

> And as the days pass,
> and the winter turns to fall,
> I hope to find you
> with me through-

Dru   *(A bad chord.)* Damn!

(The Narrator turns to the audience. She does not speak. She prefers to let the action tell the story. She sits onstage on the periphery of the ensemble and observes. The actor's break tableau as each speaks to the audience.)

Sonya It's impossible to describe what it was like. It was horrible, beyond horrible, everybody knows that. But it wasn't just like a day, or two days, and we were all just fine again. It was day after day of horrible things. Months. It felt like purgatory. Worse. In a situation like that you have to become numb. There's only so much hurt you can take. How can you describe something like that? You can't. There's no words. I…I'll never forget the things that happened, and I've tried, trust me. It still feels like some surreal dream. I had gone up to the city to get my grandmother. Also, I volunteer there at the hospital. My mom and I got my grandmother, but then Mom and I stayed after the evacuation because people were needed for evac duty at the hospital. We had put my grandmother on a bus to Houston, she was safe and on her way out, so we figured she was fine. After the hurricane hit we were put on lockdown at the hospital. A Guardsman came in a few days in, and told us he had seen our grandmother ill up at the Dome. He said she was vomiting, which is not good if you don't have the ability to rehydrate. We didn't have water in the hospital so I knew they probably didn't at the Dome. It was so hot. The same soldier ignored his orders and shuttled us over there to see if we could find her. There were heroes in all of that. He knew we were desperate. I wish I knew his name. *(A beat.)* I will never forget what I saw on the way there. The boat ride… Never. I stopped counting bodies after 6. The smell. Dead dogs. Dead people. If Hell has a river I've ridden on it. At some point I remember closing my eyes. My mother screamed. I opened them, looked over, and saw this little boy. Probably only like five.

Maybe four. It was hard to tell. Dead. Face up. His eyes were still open. He looked really dead but really alive at the same time. He was tied to a streetlamp by his foot so he wouldn't float away. God. I... *(Pauses.)* That's the first time I ever saw my mother cry. The last too. I can't even... *(Pauses.)* How do you forget that? When we got to the Dome we did eventually find my grandmother. She was dead too. We don't even know how she got off the bus. At least we found her. At least we know. You'd think it couldn't get worse than that. It did. I don't care what "authorities" say didn't happen in the Dome. I saw things happen to people that should never...I saw good people turn evil. There's no other word for it. Hell can't be worse. My grandmother...I couldn't grieve. *(Pauses.)* How do you grieve when you have no food, no water, no money, no nothing? Just numb. Some sort of survival thing kicks in and you go on autopilot. I was a zombie. I don't think I felt anything for months, but when it hit me it hit me so hard. I totally cracked. I mean cracked. I don't think I'll ever be the same. I feel like most of me is still missing. I'm definitely different. How could I be the same? How could any of us be? It didn't have to happen. None of it did. That's the thing, it didn't *(She stops.)* I... *(Pauses, gathers herself.)* It's a lot harder letting go of someone when you know they didn't have to die. I miss her. She's also what keeps me going too. God, she was such a strong woman. She lived strong and I'm sure she died strong. I know that much. That little boy though. God, my heart still breaks for him. I wonder if he died alone? A child should never have to die alone. I pray for him every day. How do you forget that?

Tice   I don't know...When you're a photographer...wanna be a photographer...you spend your life trying to frame a moment...its essence I guess. I shot the days during and after the hurricane taking... *(Beat.)*

I think I took over nine thousand photos in just a few weeks. People. Devastation. They, I…I just kept shooting and shooting. I think it was my, like, defense mechanism. My family and I had evacuated to Baton Rouge, which had its own problems, but not like the devastation in The Bayou. While I was there I maneuvered my way into helping out with a local film crew. I just started hanging out and helping them and doing things for them. They were so consumed, things were so crazy, and I don't know if they didn't notice I didn't really belong or they didn't care. I don't know…somehow they got a hold of a media helicopter and I happened to be there at the right time. They let me on. We flew down right into the heart of the devastation. It was unbelievable. My God…I can't even… *(Pause.)* I knew it was bad but I couldn't have been prepared for it. Places that I knew of as land were gone. Just gone. People on rooftops. People dead… A lot were calling to us. Screaming…totally desperate. I…they just wanted… *(Pause.)* Help. I haven't even really talked about it. I don't know…I… Seriously, nine thousand photos. I don't know. I haven't even really looked at them. I don't think I can. I've been asked to. I don't think…don't think I can. The weird thing is…I don't know, like I said, you, a photographer, spends a life trying to frame a moment, its essence. I took nine thousand photos. At least. People. Most of them were trying to, I don't know… *(Pause.)* The situation…they were already framed, in that moment, each moment, they were trying to hold onto an essence, just hold on…I don't know. I just can't look at those pictures yet. I'm not ready to…I…I don't know. I don't…I don't know…

Roxanne   We evacuated north and stayed with my aunt in Oklahoma. The craziest thing was watching it all happen on television. I learned a lot from that. I learned that most of the country has no idea that a lot of the state is south of Baton Rouge and New Orleans. I was shocked. I kept watching and listening for news about our parish but they just kept covering New Orleans. God, it made me so angry. I love New Orleans, but if you watched the news you wouldn't have known about all the damage and suffering that was happening in The Bayou. I don't think I heard the wetlands come up once. I was like, "Hello! Why do you think everything's under water?" Finally I had to stop watching television. One morning I got on the computer at the library and visited Google Earth or something to try and get some information. Our house was completely gone. Completely. There was nothing but water. It was totally surreal. I was looking at my life…completely underwater. Gone. For good. I started screaming…in the library. Screaming and crying so loud they called the police. I totally lost it. The next day I showed my mom and dad. I wish I hadn't... After that, my parents sent me to my aunt in Arkansas so I would be in a more cheerful environment. I drove back to Louisiana instead, and volunteered doing pet rescue in the lower parishes. My parents freaked when they found out. Totally freaked. But, we were able to take our dogs with us, people going to shelters couldn't. I couldn't stop thinking about all those animals. I think secretly my mom was proud. I was totally not ready for what we found, though. There were teams of pet rescuers working and there was just no way to keep up with so many animals. Imagine seeing three dogs on a house and deciding which one you should save. How do you do that? I swear, it felt like every flooded house had a pet inside. Everybody thought they would be back home in a few days. We found so many animals. Dead. Half alive. I found this one little white mixed breed, she was completely dehydrated and stuck in the top floor of a flooded house with half a roof. She smelled like gas. The entire house was sagging from water weight. She was still so cute. She had this little braided pink collar. Definitely something a little girl had made. On the door of the room she was in it said, "Please save Hope." I checked her tag. Her name was Hope... She was on IV for days. Anti-social for weeks. She bounced back, but she was clearly changed. More skeptical and afraid I guess. I guess that's true for all of us though. Eight months later she was reunited with her owners. I got to be there. It was amazing. When that little girl saw Hope...I swear it was like eight months of pain washed away. I've never cried like that. Good tears, for once. That dog, Hope, was what was holding that little girl together for all those months. Those little moments, like that one, in all of this, held us all together. In all of the horribleness there were like these little moments, glimmers, of connection. Without those, I don't think there'd be anything left to us. Each other is all we have to depend on now.

Jackie   People think folks down here didn't want to evacuate. That's stupid. How do you evacuate if your family doesn't have twenty dollars in their pocket? Poor people can't evacuate. That's for rich people. We can't just pick up and split. It's not that easy. The idea of a mandatory evacuation is bullshit. How can you make something mandatory if not everyone has the money to do it? We had no choice but to stay. It's cool though. It ended up being the best time of my life. Really. A good time. Stuck in a hot attic with five people and a dog. Shitting in a can. No food. No water. Fighting for air. Your entire life flooded two feet underneath you. Hoping your granddad doesn't die in front of you. Watching your mom go nuts. Being forced to leave your dog behind. Living in four different shelters over the next two month. Yeah, we totally didn't want to evacuate. We're rich actually, we just though all that would be fun. Word.

Thoreau   I don't talk about it. Not the personal stuff. I can't. It just kills me. I'm really sorry. None of us really talk about it. It's kind of weird that we're all going through this stuff and we don't talk about it. What I will tell you is that it was a monumental systematic failure. The biggest in American history. A social failure. A political failure. A legal failure. From the causes to the immediate impact to the residual effects. A natural disaster my ass. I loved how after the hurricane the government played the whole "this couldn't have been anticipated" game. Study after study had been published showing the relationship between the wetlands disintegration, land loss, potential levee failures, and the relative loss of thousands of lives in the event of a category four or five. If you go back and read the reports they sound like a prophecy. All of it came true. Everything. The government and the Corps had this information for years and did nothing. Then, the gall to deceive the public and behave like it was all a surprise. And then, to start finger- pointing!? The worst part is their failure to take any responsibility whatsoever, or to issue even the smallest apology. That, of course would be an admission of guilt which would open them up to lawsuits. I don't know what it will take to begin mending. The scientific solutions are present. We'll never get to them, though, until some responsibility is taken. Fucking bullshit. *(A beat.)* Sorry. I just can't talk about the personal stuff though. I hope that's okay.

Dru   My uncle was in the hospital with liver cancer. We were visiting him when the evacuation started. We knew it was coming. You could feel it. There was lots of confusion over what was happening with patients like him, so we didn't want to evacuate. We couldn't just leave him. After we checked on him-me, my mom, my dad, and my brother went home to prepare. We boarded up, collected all the food and water we could, and prayed. Yeah, I know, I'm not much of a pray-er. I prayed. Whatever. That night it hit. The whole house shook. Water started pouring in and the roof was caving…windows were blowing out. The front door ripped off and flew through the wall into the hall where we were hiding. It was like the *Amityville Horror.* The original, not the piece of shit re-make. My mother said the Holy Spirit was directing us to leave. I think the holy shits were directing us more than the Holy Spirit, but whatever, we got the hell out. I don't know how, but we made it to a shelter in Houma where we stayed for days, then we were with a family in Texas for three months. It had to be an oil family. The fucking irony in that. We located my uncle at a hospital in Florida a few weeks after the storm. I guess the holy shits were looking out for us. We would have died for sure if we had stayed. I had a lot of time to reflect and write music while I was in Texas. Every once in a while I would watch television until it pissed me off too much. It made me keep thinking, "Why are we talking about a war overseas? Why are we there? We're spending billions of dollars fighting a war over there while we have a war going on in our own country." What those billions could do here. They could have prevented the whole thing if they were used to fix the situation here before the hurricane. The real war is here. The oil is here too if that's what we're after. It didn't matter though. The government was too busy playing chess in the East to care that its own people were dying at war here. It's baffling. This wouldn't have happened in Massachusetts or Michigan.

Ronnie	It's all such a blur. I actually can't remember anything. I suppose I'm blocking it, but I really can't remember anything. I remember we finally got to a shelter in Baton Rouge. I remember I got really sick and had to be hospitalized. It was like the worst flu ever. I was really feverish, like 103. Throwing up violently, and really out of it. On top of that I think I was just dead emotionally. We had already been through hell. Lying in the hospital, I was kind of hoping I would die. I could never kill myself, it's not in me. But at that time, everything was so awful. I remember closing my eyes and praying that when I opened them I would be dead. I remember opening them and being like, well crap, then I'd try again. I do remember the weirdest thing though. I remember hearing all these seagulls outside from my hospital room. In Baton Rouge. I was so out of it, but that I remember. Vividly. I just remember thinking, "Why the hell are there so many seagulls in Baton Rouge? Aren't we too far inland? Is that much coastland gone? Is everything gone?" I kept thinking, "There shouldn't be so many seagulls here, somebody do something!" It's all a blur. I'm not sure now what was real and what wasn't. The seagulls though, they were real.
Chad	I'm sure you've heard all sorts of horror stories about the hurricane. Unless you were here, and thank God you weren't, no story will be enough for you to know what it was like. We lost our house. That's not original. Insurance fucked us. That's not original either. Fuckers. We were actually lucky. Nobody in my family died. It's all pretty fucked. I'm not gonna bore you with our problems, I'm sure you've heard it more eloquently from other people. For me, it was all the hurt and feelings of rejection that was happening underneath the everyday shit that made it so bad. I was doing this internal battle, I guess, coming to

terms that I wasn't right about everything and that my country has some serious fucking issues. It put my whole identity into question. I still love my country. I'm still ready to serve, and lay down my life if necessary. I am. I believe in its core, its values, and its purpose as a world leader. But I…after the hurricane, I was…I couldn't believe how the government had let us down…is still letting us down. Did you watch television? The bullshit that went down while people here suffered? It was unbelievable how clueless and selfish our government was during all that. It made a lot of things clear for me. I was suddenly embarrassed that I had gone to bat so many times in defense of this government's values, and even offered my life service, but to what? To a country that's ignoring its own people in need? I was just embarrassed, and ashamed, I guess. I've worn national pride on my sleeve like a badge of honor. My dad was a soldier. So was my grandfather…Korea, Vietnam, Desert Storm. I was hurt. I love this country. Look, if you were in love with somebody so much that you were willing to lay down your life for them, then one day you find out that it was all a lie, that they didn't really love you as much as you love them, that would hurt right? That's what it feels like. Am I still proud to serve? Yes. There are people in this world who need us, and I think in the end the core values that created this country…every single citizen will matter again. I believe that. Not just the rich ones. That's what all the bullshit is really about, right? Money. Politics. It's the poor and the working class that are getting fucked in all this. I won't fight for that country. That's not America. I'll fight for the America that gave birth to the Constitution and the one that I think we'll be again. I have to believe that. If I thought America has truly become what this experience has shown it to be, my entire life, and the life of my father and grandfather would all be bullshit. I always defended the Corps… the facts were all there, they just ignored them? Why? That's the question. How did money and politics become more important than people? Yeah, all the facts will come out, but I know now the Corps holds some of the blame. They failed us. That's definite. You have no idea how much it sucks for me to admit that. It tears me up.

(The ensemble is reflective as they speak.)

Renee   It's impossible to describe what it was like.

Thomas   It felt like purgatory.

Tricia   You have to become numb.

LeDeux   There's only so much hurt you can take before it just numbs you.

Saranda   How can you describe something like that?

Mich & LeD You can't.

Ronnie   It was a monumental systematic failure.

Chad   I'll never forget the things that happened.

Thoreau   It still feels like some surreal dream.

Jackie   I will never forget the things that I saw.

Tice   Just numb.

Roxanne   I don't think I'll ever be the same.

Dru   I feel like most of me is still missing.

Thomas   It didn't have to happen.

Michelle   None of it did. That's the thing-

Thor & Son It didn't have to happen.

Jackie   That's the thing.

Ronnie   They let us down.

Chad   If we still had our wetlands maybe no one would have died.

Renee   Each other is all we really have to depend on.

Dru & Tric How could we be the same?

Sonya   How could any of us be?

(A loud siren interrupts.)

Voice-Over   Attention. This is a hurricane education alert. This is a hurricane-

Ensemble   *(Except Celia.)* Shut up!!!!

(It stops. Silence.)

Celia.   Evangeline found herself alone in a new world, full of uncertainty, her love dashed by the cruelty of consequence and geography. Days turned to weeks. Weeks turned to seasons. But Gabriel did not come. Seasons turned to years and still no word. Evangeline's heart grew tired, but she refused to give up hope. She turned her time to the church and to others who had fallen victim to the hurricane. One day, while Evangeline was at a church mission in a neighboring village, a young girl approached her with news of Gabriel. He was dead.

(The ensemble looks at Celia. They now understand her story is about she and JD. The Narrator takes note, clearly impacted by this development. They all listen.)

It was rumored that he had fallen ill and died while returning home in the months following the hurricane. Upon hearing of his death, Evangeline's love of Gabriel turned to deep grief. She thought of ending

her life, but turned her despair into devotion for
God. *(A beat. Her story moves to the future.)* She
decided to move to a western parish and take her
religious vows, and dedicate the remainder of her
life to providing for the poor and to soothing the
pain of the sick and dying. After many decades of
reverential devotion, she found herself an old woman
with hair the color of a grey sky, and a life filled with
the colors of the Lord. Evangeline had become well-
loved and respected for her charity, yet a part of her
still quietly mourned for Gabriel. She also mourned,
with a twinge of responsibility, for the loss of heritage
and family tradition that had died with her father
years earlier. She prayed daily for a... *(Thinking.)*
A solution to her spiritual conflict. *(Writes.)* A
solution...

Narrator   *(To the ensemble.)* Is there a solution?

Thoreau   *(Definitively.)* Yes.

Michelle   Is there?

Tice   Yes.

Thoreau   Yeah, there are lots of solutions, that's part of the
problem. There's been this shotgun approach to fixing
things.

Michelle   Yep.

Thoreau   There's no organization, no central way of getting
anything done. Typical politics. Here's the great thing
and the horrible thing about the hurricane. On one
hand it brought us forward like fifty years. Finally
people are like "Holy crap, people dying from what?
I thought they just ran round drunk and flashing their
tits." So, we finally have the country's attention.
On the other hand, most people on the outside still
don't understand that it's a wetlands problem. The

	devastation from the hurricane wasn't a natural disaster. I'll say it again. It was not a natural disaster! People think, "Oh, let's just rebuild."
Tice	"Bigger levees."
Thoreau	How often do we hear that? Like that's all we need.
Narr	I've heard it often.
Thoreau	It's one part. If we rebuild without a wetlands barrier guess what's gonna happen next time? Exact same thing. Probably worse. If this country has any interest in protecting its resour-
Saranda	We *are* a resource.
Thoreau	Something has got to be done to fix the wetlands.
Narr	What?
Dru	Remember how horrible 9/11 was?
Renee	Oh, don't go there please.
Dru	I'm going there. 9/11 was un-Godly horrible and the whole country reacted right? What's happening here is not that different except the terrorists are on the inside, and they're shaking hands with our politicians.
Jackie	Some of them *are* our politicians.
Renee	Please! C'mon. Are you really gonna throw some conspiracy thing into this?
Dru	It's not a conspiracy. I'm not saying it's that. But, our government knows what is happening, the energy companies know what is happening, but it's still happening. Are they doing anything? Sure, they're fucking shaking hands at dinner parties! If you're contributing to an entire part of the country

being destroyed you're a terrorist. *(Getting heated.)* Wouldn't you call that terrorism?

Tice   *(Joking.)* Are they gonna start profiling white guys in three-piece suits?

Dru   They should.

Ronnie   Culture's are disappearing. *(To Narrator.)* Isn't that, like, some sort of social genocide?

LeDeux   *(Not wanting it to go there.)* Baseball.

Ronnie   Seriously. Think of what's happening…what we're losing…

Narr   Heritage?

Tricia   Music... Cajun, Zydeco, Blues—

Sonya   *(Partly joking.)* Grandma's gumbo!

Michelle   History.

LeDeux   Um, baseball!

Chad   Baseball is fine. How about energy resources?

Saranda   We're like a third of the country's oil.

Jackie   Petro yo.

Chad   This country hasn't even come close to seeing high gas prices.

Renee   Just wait.

Ronnie   No crap…our impact on the rest of the country… nobody outside of The Bayou cares though, do they? I mean *really*? This country cares about money. That's what got us into this mess. Does anyone outside of Louisiana know we also supply like a third of the country's seafood? And our ports…stuff that you buy in, like, a New Jersey Wal-Mart comes in through *our* ports. Computers, socks, coffee, condoms, whatever. When we're gone-

Dru   They don't use condoms in Jersey.

(Laughs. A few fist pumps from the group.)

Narr   What about natural resources?

Dru   Wetlands.

Roxanne   Endangered wildlife.

Jackie   That's us, wet and wild, bitches.

Ronnie   Here's the thing. This is not a Louisiana problem.

Chad   This is a national problem, a social problem.

Sonya   *(Overlapping Chad.)* A social problem.

(An aha moment. Sonya and Chad smile.)

Narr   Solutions?

Thoreau   Yes.

Narr   Tell me.

Tricia   *Better* levees?

Dru   Education.

LeDeux   Floodable construction.

Michelle   Corporate regulation.

Roxanne   Communication.

Jackie   *(Joking.)* What?

(Roxanne gives him the hand.)

Ronnie   Activism. Political reform.

Sonya	People think their vote doesn't matter.
Tice	Does it?
Saranda	No. Wetlands restoration.
Thoreau	Restoration. Sure. That's actually the easy part.
Dru	Close ALL the fucking man-made canals. Just say no to Mr. Go!
Ensemble	Just say no to Mr. Go!!

(Now they're having fun with it.)

Jackie	Yeah bitches!
Tricia	Sustainable energy.
Tice	Tax penalties!
Saranda	Yeah! Hit 'em in the wallet!
Chad	Hold politicians' feet to the fire!
Ronnie	Hold them accountable!
Roxanne	For once.
Michelle	Stop earmarks.
Tricia	Reward sustainable industry practices!
Renee	Fuck Yeah!
Dru	Fuck Yeah!
All	Fuck Yeah!!

(Laughs.)

Thomas	*(Jokingly.)* This has been a "learnable moment."

(Some ironic laughs. They've all heard that many times.)

Narr	In all sincerity, you are the most socially informed teenagers I've ever met.
Michelle	It's not a choice.
Narr	Do you think people on "the outside" know what you're going through?

(Long beat. A hopelessness in their silence.)

Thoreau	Look, we're like a, *(searching for the right word)* a sentinel for the whole country right now. How the country handles the wetlands issues here…I think it'll determine the future of our whole country. It puts our priorities into question, doesn't it? People or money? Like my dad always says, "The right thing is never easy."
Thomas	*(Half jokingly.)* I know someone who would completely agree with that. *(Meaning Jesus.)*
Dru	Oh Jesus. *(An ironic choice of words.)*
Thomas	Exactly. Look, if you had one message to learn from Jesus' life what would it be?

(A beat.)

LeDeux	Don't play hide the boudin with thy neighbor's wife?
Thomas	Funny, but no. Not just his teachings, but his *life*… what would the message be?

(A few beats.)

Jackie	Jesus is my homeboy?
Michelle	*(To Jackie and LeDeux.)* Really guys?
Thomas	Think about it…Jesus showed us that making the right choice, the right moral choice, is the hardest, but in the end it's the one that provides you with redemption, right? With a new beginning. With

salvation. *(Pleased.)* Damn, I think I just found my first sermon.

Tricia   Can Priests say damn?

Thomas   Priests invented the word. Can I read something? *(He reads.)* "We rejoice in our sufferings because we know that suffering produces perseverance, character, and character, hope. And hope does not disappoint us." Romans. *(Looks to Chad.)* The right thing is never easy.

Chad   Tell my parents that.

Ronnie   But it is easier, *because* it's right.

Jackie   *(Commenting on the direction of the conversation, he sings.)* "Kumbaya my Lord, Kumbaya."

Dru   *(To Jackie.)* Hush.

Saranda   It's true. He's right. It's like…It's like… *(Searching for the metaphor.)* Ok. I got it. When I had Aiden my grandma was like, "If it don't hurt, something ain't right." Right? "It's gotta hurt to make a life." Make sense?

LeDeux   Nope.

Sonya   Oh my God. Do you know how much the pregnancy rate went up right after the hurricane? Kind of weird that all this crap happens then *more* babies are born. *(To Narr.)* What d'ya call that?

Narr   I don't know.

Dru   Fucked up.

Thoreau   I'll make it my first book. *"Post Catastrophic Regeneration in Bayou Country."*

Chad   "Gettin' a Hump Start."

(Laughs.)

Saranda   *(To Chad.)* Seriously?

LeDeux   Uh….it's called having a giant boner and being stuck in a shelter for a month.

Renee   Must y'all kill everything beautiful?!

LeDeux   I'm a realist. That's how I "sustain" myself. Ha, did you hear that? "Sustain." Tossing around the lingo… Crack! Rahhhhh!! *(He's hit another home run.)*

(A loud class bell rings. They rise and abruptly move to "drama class.")

Roxanne   All right you guys. Rehearsal time. C'mon, move! Stop talking. Let's-

Tice   *(Mocking her.)* "Stop talking."

Roxanne   Move it. C'mon! Please shut up. We gotta read through this skit.

Chad   This shit?

Roxanne   Skit. SKit! Please don't make me kick your ass! *(To all.)* C'mon guys!

(Roxanne hands out scripts. General improvisation. The ensemble prepares to enter into a read-through of a skit, a mock post-hurricane political debate. The Narrator sits and watches. Roxanne will read the part of "a host." "A president" is read by LeDeux. Tice is to read the part of "a mayor," and Ronnie is to read the part of "an environmental leader." The rest of the ensemble are "members of the press," except Celia, who continues to write.)

Host   *(Reading.)* Ladies and gentlemen of the viewing audience. The Drama Club is proud to sponsor this very special occasion. On stage with us tonight will be three important figures coming together to debate the hurricane recovery process. Our panelists this evening include: *(Pointing to the actor reading each role as she states the part.)* a leader in the environmental movement *(Ronnie playfully gives a peace sign.)*, the Mayor of a prominent city in southeast Louisiana-

Tice *(As self.)* That's me bitches.

Roxanne *(Ignoring him.)*…and a President of the United States. *However, there is a twist. (An aside to "audience.")* Unbeknownst to our participants, after each question I will award a point to the one that provides the worst answer. The one with the greatest number of worst answer points after ten questions will receive an all-expense paid trip to the town of Bite My Ass, Louisiana. Now let's give them a warm welcome.

(Roxanne gestures to Tice, Ronnie, and LeDeux to stand. Applause from "press.")

Good evening and welcome. First question panelists. How is the hurricane recovery progressing? We'll begin with you, Mr. President.

(A pause.)

Roxanne *(To LeDeux, who is busy licking his lips at Renee.)* Hello!?.

LeDeux Oh shiii… *(Reads from script. Doing his best presidential voice.)* Ahem. I'd first like to remind all the people affected by the hurricane how important it is to stay in school, especially those ones that might not have a school anymore.

Thomas *(As himself.)* Guys, this already isn't funny.

Roxanne *(As herself.)* Chill out please. Keep reading.

LeDeux	*(As President.)* Now, I'd say were doing a damn fine job down here. Sure, we got a little rebuilding to do... but out of that re-building chaos is going to come a really fantastic new Gulf Coast, almost as good as it was before...
Thomas	Seriously. Not funny.
Jackie	He's right, it's not funny. Dis ain't funny, bitches.
Chad	It's freakin' hilarious, what're you even talking about?
Saranda	He's right. Why the hell are we joking about this?
Ronnie	Seriously.
Tricia	It's not funny.
Chad	Oh my God, loosen up.
Tice	*(To Ronnie.)* "Seriously."
Dru	Relax.
Jackie	*(Singing.)* "Don't do it, when you wanna suck to it."
LeDeux	That's not even rap, it's gay pop.
Jackie	You would know.
LeDeux	Your mother would know.
Jackie	*(Mocking him.)* "Your mother would know."
Michelle	He's right, we shouldn't be laughing at this-
Renee	It's not making anything better.
Chad	It's making *me* feel better.
Renee	Whatever.
Chad	It's not making anything worse.
Tice	It's funny.

Renee   It's not.

Tice   *(Mocking her.)* Is too.

Michelle   Stop it guys.

Chad   Be quiet. Please! *(Catching their attention.)* Look...
            (Sincerely.) If I don't laugh, I'll fucking scream.

Roxanne   Then scream.

Chad   No. That's gay.

Ronnie   Can you pick a different word?

Chad   *(Lashing at her.)* Retarded?

Roxanne   Just scream. Do it. Do it. C'mon. *(She yells in his
            face.)* Aaagghh!

Chad   No! It's stupid.

Roxanne   Do it. *(Yelling.)* Do it, soldier!

Thomas   Do it!

Ensemble   Do it! Do it! Do it! *(They repeat many times, building
            to a loud chant.)*

Chad   *(He screams gently.)* Aaagghh!

Roxanne   Louder.

Chad   *(Louder.)* Aaaaaggghhh!!!

Roxanne   C'mon. Everybody!

            (Some join in. Tricia and Celia do not.)

Ensemble   Agggghhhhhhh!

Roxanne   C'mon!! *(To all.)* Scream. Screeeeam!!

            (More join in.)

Ensemble   Arrgghhhhhhh!

Roxanne   Louder!

Ensemble   Aaarrrggggghhhhhh!

(All are now screaming, except for Celia and Tricia. It turns into a great screaming improvisation. They scream at each other, scream at the sky, scream at the ground, etc. Celia is still writing. Tricia moves to her guitar. Screaming, others start to involve their bodies. It grows and grows. It reaches the point of ridiculous, becomes hysterical. A great release. The screamers all end up on the floor, laughing. After a bit, the laughing begins to subside.)

Roxanne   Excellent. And…breathe! *(Ending her acting exercise, she directs them to inhale deeply, then exhale.)*

(Upon her direction, they let out a collective vocal sigh. Resting on each other, holding hands, etc., they stay in silence. They reflect. As Thomas settles he is stopped by Celia's voice.)

Celia.   *(To herself.)* Shoot!

(She is having problems as she nears the end of the story.)

(Reading.) …had become well loved and respected for her charity, yet a part of her still quietly, desperately, mourned for Gabriel. She also mourned, with a twinge of responsibility, for the loss of the heritage and family tradition that had died with her father years earlier… No. *(Struggling for the words.)*…she mourned deeply for her loss… No. Despite her love for God she mourned for her earthly loss… No. Guised under her reverent attire was an earthly loss, deep and confounding… Darn. Her loss weighed upon her like an icy January… No. That's terrible. Despite her deep love for the Lord, she felt desperately alone in the world. *(She got it.)*

Thomas   Celia. That's really good.

Celia   Thanks.

Thomas   How's it gonna end?

(She is silent. Thomas looks at her, then joins others on floor. The Narrator considers the question- "How is it gonna end?"- then exits gently.)

(Tricia plays guitar and sings. "Someday." The song is complete. Others remain on floor.)

Tricia   It's kinda late
but I'm not sleeping.
A million thoughts in my head,
keep me awake
as I lay seeking,
the key to my piece of mind.
My fame my glory,
written like a bedtime story,
with an ending that is happy every time.
Cus I used to dream instead of thinking,
and I would follow my heart,
sailing the seas instead of sinking,
into an ocean of pride,
losing my patience,
trapped inside my own frustrations,
feeling like I might of missed the chance to try.
And even though I'm closer
than I've ever been before
the future seems a million miles away,
but I can't stop now,
I won't know how
til I reach the moon some day,
and I'll reach the moon some day.
And even though I'm closer
than I've ever been before
the future seems a million miles away,

but I can't stop now,
I won't know how
til I reach the moon some day,
and I'll reach the moon some day.
I'll see you when I pass the milky way.
Cus I'll reach the moon some day.

Tricia   *(Speaking to her unseen mother.)* Mom, I'm gonna go
             to bed. Okay, goodnight. Yeah, I love you too.

*(Tricia exits as if going to bed. Others follow Tricia's
lead. One by one, those on the floor begin saying their
goodnights to their families as if they are at home. They
rise and exit stage as they say goodnight. Celia stays
behind.)*

Renee   Goodnight, Mom. Yeah. I will, I will. Seven. Yes,
             seven *a.m.* Got it. Good night.

Ronnie   Mom, I got it done. Love you too. Yeah. I'll drive her
             in. Night, Grandma.

Michelle   Goodnight.

Roxanne   I'm hittin' the hay. You too. I said you too. Okay…
             love ya.

Chad   See you on the flip side.

Thomas   Night, Dad.

Saranda   I will. Don't forget I need the car tomorrow. Yeah, I
             gotta bring him by after school. I will.

Sonya   Love you too. Sweet dreams.

Thoreau   Mom. Can you leave the gas money on the table?
             Thanks. G'night.

LeDeux   Ugghh. I'm so beat. Hey, do we have eggs left? Cool.
             Okay, goodnight.

Tice	Yes, I set it. I double checked. *(Jokingly.)* Night Ma, night Pa, night John Boy.
Dru	Don't forget to wake me up. Um, I told you that. It hasn't worked for like, a week. Okay.
Jackie	I love you too. Sleep tiiigght.
Ensemble	Goodnight.

(Celia is left alone onstage. She reads the end of her Evangeline adaptation.)

Celia   One spring day in her 78th year, Evangeline traveled to meet with a dying old man in a northern parish. Along the way she picked magnolia flowers to brighten his spirits. It is said in Acadian culture that the magnolia flower has the power to keep a person afloat, as long as they have the strength to keep it within their grasp. Finding herself weary after a day of traveling, she decided to lodge in a local seminary outside of the town where the man had fallen ill. That night, she dreamt of Gabriel. She…she dreamt of the life they would have created together, and of the children and grandchildren that they would have raised…raised in the proud traditions of their cultures.

(Lights begin to dim.)

She awoke with the sensation of floating between two worlds, full of God's heavenly devotion…empty from the loss of her earthly love. She said a prayer to quiet her internal conflict, picked up the magnolias, and traveled to the hospital where the man resided. She entered his room. He was a gaunt old man, skeletal as the dying cypress, but he held a glint of heavenly serenity in his eyes. The magnolia flowers dropped from her hands, for, in a dreamlike halo of sunlight, his weathered face seemed young. Evangeline recognized him. It was Gabriel. Without words, she

sat beside him, and lifted his head to her heart. She
wept. They looked into each other's eyes, smiled, and
with his last breath Gabriel whispered, "My wife."
His eyes closed. Evangeline gently returned his head
to the pillow, lay down beside him, and placed her
own head upon his heart. It was silent. She softly
whispered "I love you, my husband," closed her eyes,
and died

*(Lights continue to dim. Celia places a small handgun on
the floor beside her.)*

Gabriel and Evangeline. Their earthbound journey
finished, now re-united, their souls bound under the
graceful hand of God. Their homeland disintegrated,
their culture vanished, and the lineage of their
families…dead.

*(Lights have gone extremely dim. Celia tries a different
variation.)*

Gabriel and Evangeline, young lovers grown old,
drowned in life by the consequen…

(She scratches out that last sentence.)

Gabriel and Evangeline…a story of young hope who
only in death, found their love... ...their life. Once
upon a time. (She writes two final words, "The End,"
but does not say them aloud. A moment.)*

*(She has completed it. Lights to full black. A loud gunshot.
She has killed herself.)*

*(Responding to the shot, Thomas quickly enters and
discovers her. Lights rise. Knowing she's dead, he sits
beside her and prays. A magnolia flower falls gently from
above. Thomas takes solemn notice of it.)*

(The ensemble layers in, fixed on Celia's body.)

Ronnie	*(To self.)* My God. *(Picks up Celia's book. Sits. Reads the last words.)* ..."A story of young hope who only in death, found their love...their life. Once upon a time.
	The end."

(The ensemble's lines may gently overlap in the following dialogue as immediacy and line continuity demands.)

Thomas	No.
Tice	The End?!
Renee	How can it be the end?
Chad	It can't be.
Thoreau	Doesn't make sense.
Roxanne	It was supposed to be once upon a time.
LeDeux	Once upon a fucking time.
Dru	Fuck!
Tricia	She's fifteen.
Ren & Son	Fuck this!!
Michelle	Why is this happening?
Saranda	Why?
Chad	This didn't have to happen.
Thomas	Didn't?
Jackie	This doesn't have to happen.
Thoreau	No.
Tricia	This isn't once upon a time.
Dru & Ron	This is now.

Tice	This is here.
LeDeux	This isn't happening.
Roxanne	It isn't?
Sonya	Yes. It is.
Michelle	This is happening.
Thomas	She's a good kid.
LeDeux	Us too.
Saranda	Good freaking kids.
Jack & Tric	Good people.
Chad	Ahhhhggghh!
Thoreau	What're we supposed to do?
Tice	Where are the people who are supposed to help?
Thomas	Where?
Thoreau	Are they.
Son & Sar	What are we supposed to do?
Ronnie	Where is *our* hope?
Jackie	Our glint of heavenly serenity…
Michelle	Where is our comfort?
Renee	Living comfort?
Thomas	Dying.
Jackie	Look at her.
Son & LeD	Look at us!

(Some of the dialogue becomes directed at the audience.)

Roxanne   Look.

Saranda   Please.

Michelle   Listen.

Chad   Listen harder.

Thom & Ren Listen!!!

Saranda   Please. *(A beat.)* Please.

Jackie   Just.

Sonya   Listen.

Michelle   Please.

Dru   Please God.

Roxanne   We're.

Ronnie   Hurting.

Tricia   We're.

Roxanne   Hoping.

LeDeux   We're.

Ren & Thor Alone.

Chad   Losing Faith.

Renee   In America.

Sonya   Losing faith.

Thomas   In God.

Tricia   Losing faith in myself.

Tice   Already lost it.

Thoreau   Fucking angry!

Michelle   Confused.

Jack & Dru Waiting.

Renee   Waiting.

Roxanne   Under the cypress.

Chad   Skeletal.

Saranda   We're losing our homes.

Thomas   Lost.

Jackie   Sinking.

Sonya   Sunk.

Dru & Mich Our families.

Ronnie   Eroding.

Tric & Rox Gone.

Saranda   Our friends.

Tice   Falling.

Renee   Apart.

LeDeux   Our culture.

Chad   AWOL.

Thoreau   Holding.

Ron & Sar   Holding on...

Sonya   ...holding the magnolia.

Tricia   The magnolia.

Dru   Gabriel.

Renee   JD.

Roxanne   Evangeline.

Jackie   Celia.

Tice   Gasping.

Thomas   Slowly...

Chad   Drowning.

Mich, Sar, & Son   Drowning.

(A beat.)

Ronnie   ...Evangeline drowning. *(She reverently puts down Celia's book.)*

(Each walks slowly DS and lights a white candle. Tricia and Dru carry their candles to the piano and begin playing/ singing. Others form a slow procession. During the song, Celia's body is carried through the house by LeDeux, followed by the candle procession, all behind her body as in a solemn funeral march. LeDeux exits with Celia's body but the others move to the periphery/voms of the house.)

Tricia & Dru *(Singing "Through it All." Dru plays. It is completed.)*

> I hope to find you,
> on a snowy winter morn,
> laughing beside me
> on a bed that's soft and warm.
> And as the days pass,
> and the winter turns to fall,
> I hope to find you
> with me through it all.
> I hope to find you,
> on a glowing summer day,
> walking beside me
> as the shadows fade away.
> And as the days pass,

and the summer turns to fall,
I hope to find you
with me through it all.
Let the walls come down.
Take a look around and you'll find
if together we should stay,
cause even though today,
as our lives change
and it feels like we may fall,
I stand beside you
with you through it all.
Let the walls come down.
Take a look around and you'll find
if together we should stay.
Cause even though today,
as our lives change
and it feels like we may fall,
I stand beside you
with you through it all.
I hope to find you
with me through it all.

(Tricia, Dru, and LeDeux, with lit candles, join ensemble on the periphery/voms of the house.)

Thomas	Once upon a time, there was a boy.
Jackie	A young man.
Michelle	A girl.
Renee	A young woman.
Saranda	Growing up too quickly.
Chad	Managing the hurt.
Tice	Navigating the road ahead.
Ronnie	Proud of her heritage.

LeDeux   Scared for his future.

(Narrator re-enters with two lit candles. She puts them down and picks up Celia's journal.)

Narr   Once upon a time. Our children's future held promise. *(A beat, looks at them.)* The future… *(Looks at Tricia.)* The future held…

(Before each following phrase a magnolia flower falls gently from above the actor. After each phrase, the actor blows out his/her candle.)

Tricia   Tricia. *(A magnolia flower falls.)* A Grammy-award winning vocalist. *(Blows candle out.)*

(The Narrator reads the following dialogue from Celia's journal.)

Narr   In a wetland primeval

Renee   Renee. *(A magnolia flower falls.)* A community leader and pioneer for political reform. *(Blows candle out.)*

Narr   The murmuring oaks and naked cypress

Jackie   Jackie. *(A magnolia flower falls.)* CEO of Sony Entertainment. *(Blows candle out.)*

Narr   Once bearded with moss

Thomas   Thomas. *(A magnolia flower falls.)* Parish Priest. *(Blows candle out.)*

Narr   And in garments green

Dru   Dru. *(A magnolia flower falls.)* Youth counselor. *(Blows candle out.)*

Narr   Now skeletal in the twilight

Michelle   Michelle. *(A magnolia flower falls.)* Professor of Economics, Columbia University *(Blows candle out.)*

Narr	Stand proud and stubborn like dying cultures of old
Ronnie	Ronnie. *(A magnolia flower falls.)* Noted author and community activist. *(Blows candle out.)*
Narr	With voices sad and prophetic
Chad	Chad. *(A magnolia flower falls.)* Decorated veteran. Founder, Army Corps Office for Environmental Sustainability. *(Blows candle out.)*
Narr	While the deep voiced creatures within
Sonya	Sonya. *(A magnolia flower falls.)* Head nurse in a children's psychiatric ward. *(Blows candle out.)*
Narr	Sing a guttural funeral march
Roxanne.	Roxanne. *(A magnolia flower falls.)* Actress. Spokesperson for the World Wildlife Federation. *(Blows candle out.)*
Narr	The encroaching Gulf also speaks And in accents disconsolate answers their wails
Thoreau	Thoreau. *(A magnolia flower falls.)* Biologist. Author of NY Times Best Seller, *How We Saved Our Wetlands: The Untold Story. (Blows candle out.)*
Narr	This is the wetlands primeval proudly dying And here are the hearts that within it live
Saranda	Saranda. *(A magnolia flower falls.)* Mother. Grandmother. *(Blows candle out.)*
Narr	They now leap like the fawn
Tice	Tice. *(A magnolia flower falls.)* Award-winning photojournalist. *(Blows candle out.)*
Narr	When they hear the call of the Gulf

LeDeux   LeDeux. *(A magnolia flower falls.)* Second baseman
          for a new MLB franchise, the Louisiana Pride. *(Blows
          candle out.)*

          *(The Narrator puts Celia's journal down. She picks up the
          two lit candles.)*

Narr   JD. *(A magnolia flower falls.)* Dedicated father. "The
          shadow which swam across the marsh and found itself
          in the sunset." *(Smiles. Blows the candle out. One is
          still lit. She moves DS and sits.)*
          Once upon a time…
          (Sincerely.) This was the home of the Acadian Farmer
          The Indian Fisherman
          Of many cultures, proud and sufficient
          Of lives and love and bonds unbreakable
          Men and women whose futures glided
          on the bayous that line the wetlands
          Now darkened by the shadows
          of a destructive new world

Ensemble Once upon a time…

Narr   *(Holding up candle.)* …and Celia. *(A magnolia flower
          falls.)* Newbery Award winning children's author.
          (Blows her candle out.)

          *(The student ensemble gently exits. The child from Act I
          has emerged from the shadows US. She picks up Celia's
          writing journal from the floor and reads it aloud, gently,
          almost inaudible. Her quiet reading softly underscores the
          dialogue of Narrator below.)*

Child   …somewhere between yesterday and tomorrow,
          stands a village. Nestled in among the primeval
          swamps and majestic cypress, the village struggles
          for breath in a new world. Once bustling with life and
          flourishing with the wealth of happy subsistence, the
          village now fights the encroaching water from the
          south. The trials of poverty and the yearly beatings

of hurricanes are so frequent they now seem almost ritualistic to those hearty souls remaining there, absorbed into the identity of a people strong and willful. The village seems to float between two levees. One, a reminder of the historic past, and the other, a sign of a diminishing future. *(She pages ahead in Celia's journal.)*…Gabriel and Evangeline's childhood friendship grew into love, and at the age of 18 they found themselves planning their wedding with the excitement of life anew. In the unseen horizon, an approaching hurricane bristled and grew in power. The young lovers knew of the hurricane, but nothing could stop the joy and youthful vigor of their coming marriage. Their families gathered at Benedict's house for a party celebrating the engagement of Evangeline and Gabriel. It was the eve of their wedding. On that hot August day, the two families danced and ate and passed on old stories under the shade of the live oaks. The joyous celebration painted two beautiful portraits, one of young love, and another of the coming together of two cultures proud, colorful, and resourceful. To their families, the bond of Evangeline and Gabriel also marked the survival of cultural lineage and long held family traditions. Their love…

(The Narrator pulls out the pocket notepad that also contains CC's folded letter. References the pad.)

Narrator   *(Over the child's soft voice.)* Once upon a time…a teenager pictured her heritage… imagined her future... *(A moment. Looks at a note in the pad. Reads.)* "It's hard to imagine what it's like to grow up in a place you know is disappearing." *(A beat. Looks at another note.)* "If Hell has a river I've ridden on it." *(Beat. And another note.)* "A child should never have to die alone." *(Another.)* "If we still had our wetlands maybe no one would have died." *(Another.)* "Each other is all we have to depend on."

(A longer beat. Another note.) "Her name was Hope."
(A thoughtful beat. She unfolds CC's letter. Takes a long look at it. Shows it to the audience as she reads it.) "Please get people to help." *(Looks at audience. A moment. Not sure how to translate what she has witnessed into words. Looks at the girl. Pages to another note. Reads.)* "It could be that making the right choice is the hardest, but in the end it is the choice that provides you with a new beginning." *(A beat. Sincerely, to audience.)* We've already lost so much. We're losing… *(Checks notes.)* "Those who may literally hold the world in their hands." *(Looks to the child, who is still reading softly. A moment. Goes to notes again.)*

(Reads.) "Yet he who believes affection that hopes, and endures, and is patient
She who believes in the strength of human resilience and the beauty of love
List to this tradition still sung by the children
of this land
List to a tale of youth and hope in Acadie,
home of the brave."

(Honestly, to audience.) We are all Evangeline. *(Looks at child.)*

Child   *(Reads.)* …and their love planted a new seed of hope in the village. *(She notices a magnolia flower next to her. She picks it up. Looking back in the journal, she refers back to the beginning of the story.)* Once upon a time… *(Closes journal. Blackout.)*

For Leasing and Music Inquiries Contact:
Performance Leasing, Evangeline Drowning
evangelinedrowning@hotmail.com

About the Author

Kurt Gerard Heinlein

Kurt Gerard Heinlein is an Associate Professor of Theatre at Missouri State University where he coordinates the BFA Actor Training Program. Kurt is a working member of AEA and SAG/AFTRA. He is also an active member of The Society of American Fight Directors, Fight Directors Canada, and serves as executive leadership for The Association of Theatre Movement Educators. Kurt has performed and directed extensively since completing his MFA in Acting from the Cincinnati College-Conservatory of Music (CCM), with union performance credits that include New York, regional theatre, daytime drama, film, commercial print, and over 25 national television spots. His directing credits include New York, regional, and university theatre, and his stunt, aerial, and combat work have been seen in daytime drama, numerous national commercials, and in the professional and educational theatre circuits. Kurt completed his Ph.D. in theatre from Louisiana State University, and has been awarded several honors for his work in Green Theatre (performance that promotes socio-environmental betterment). Notable publications include *Koko and the Performance of Conservationism*, and *Green Theatre: Promoting Ecological Preservation and Advancing the Sustainability of Humanity and Nature*. In 2009, NPR dubbed Kurt "The emerging father of American Green Theatre." Kurt maintains a consistent dedication to environmental education, noted by his volunteer work for The Nature Conservancy, The National Park Service, and the SAG sponsored BookPals Literacy Program. Kurt has received several awards for his volunteerism and public service, including his work surrounding the development of *Evangeline Drowning*. Kurt is married to Courtney Heinlein and they have two wonderful children together.